THE CASTLE LECTURES
IN ETHICS, POLITICS, AND ECONOMICS

That Is Not Who We Are!

Populism and Peoplehood

ROGERS M. SMITH

Yale UNIVERSITY PRESS

New Haven and London

Yale University Press books may be purchased in quantity for educational, business, or promotional use. For information, please e-mail sales.press@yale.edu (U.S. office) or sales@yaleup.co.uk (U.K. office).

Set in Minion type by IDS Infotech Ltd.
Printed in the United States of America.

Library of Congress Control Number: 2019945877
ISBN 978-0-300-22939-4 (hardcover : alk. paper)

A catalogue record for this book is available from the British Library.

This paper meets the requirements of ANSI/NISO Z39.48-1992 (Permanence of Paper).

10 9 8 7 6 5 4 3 2 1

Parts of this book were given as the Castle Lectures in Yale's Program in Ethics, Politics, and Economics, delivered by Rogers M. Smith at Yale University in 2018.

The Castle Lectures were endowed by Mr. John K. Castle. They honor his ancestor the Reverend James Pierpont, one of Yale's original founders. Given by established public figures, Castle Lectures are intended to promote reflection on the moral foundations of society and government and to enhance understanding of ethical issues facing individuals in our complex modern society.

For Henry Dale Smith, Sr., and Betty Mood Smith

Who moved from the Land of Calhoun to the Land of Lincoln
And helped people be better everywhere

Contents

That Is Not Who We Are!

Introduction

Political leaders often tell their constituents, "That is not who we are!" or, more positively, "This is who we are!" as they seek support for their policies and power. They always have. Today, however, we seem to hear these ringing proclamations more often than ever before. We live in an era marked by highly visible, highly vocal forms of what we have come to call "identity politics"—especially, in recent years, "national identity politics."

This development may seem ironic. For many years, intellectual and sometimes political challenges to "essentialist" understandings of human identities have been on the rise. Many identities once considered natural or biological or divinely ordained, including race, ethnicity, religion, and gender, are now seen, in large part, as matters of human social and political construction, and so to some degree matters of choice. Yet the rhetoric of "this is who we are" and "that is not who we are" gains much of its force from the suggestion that the speaker is articulating the unalterable essence of our identities. The implication is that while we can *try* to see ourselves as different and to act different from who the speaker says we are, by doing so, we betray our true selves. So academic choruses of "there is *no* true, fixed 'who' that we are" proliferate alongside political choruses of "that *is* or *is not* who we are."

What are the roots of this contrast? It is always tempting to say about a difference of views that each side has part of the truth; but that is, at best, unevenly so in this case. After wrestling with empirical and normative issues of political identity and status for many years, I have concluded that the trends that advance "antiessentialist" and "constructivist" conceptions of identities and statuses are broadly right. Their real problem is that they do not go far enough. We are still only beginning to acknowledge this radical truth: every human identity is partly a product of contingent social and political construction, always working, to be sure, with preexisting biological and social materials that have finite malleability.

That still-dawning recognition has been slow in coming. The human sciences have long treated identities such as gender, race, region, religion, and class chiefly as independent variables, somehow generated in ways that do not involve human agency, which then shape politics and society. Though we have made progress in many disciplinary arenas, we still have far to go in grasping how all our identities are also dependent variables, phenomena that are substantially constituted by political and social processes, and individual choices. We are just beginning to provide theoretically and empirically persuasive accounts of how these processes and choices work in shaping all our senses of our selves.[1]

We most fall short, however, in our normative responses to this feature of the human condition. Many of us do not want to accept it, and so we are reluctant to reason morally on the basis of it. This failing contributes to the persistent essentialist tone of much contemporary political discourse, and to some of the most dangerous forms of recent politics. The fundamental reason for our reluctance to give up essentialist understandings of at least some of our identities was well expressed by that frequent sprayer of cynical acid Oliver Wendell Holmes Jr. in his greatest essay, "The Path of the Law." There Holmes wrote of the "longing for certainty and for repose which is in every human mind," while observing soberly, "But certainty generally is an illusion, and repose is not the destiny of man."[2] The heightened recognition today that none of our identities is fully natural or fixed has often frustrated longings for certainty, and it has denied many of us repose. It can seem to leave us with no place to stand, no sense of how and where to go—to make all that is solid melt into air. As a result, people across the political spectrum have long pushed against it. Many deploy, and believe in, discourses suggesting that though some of our identities are socially constructed and at least partly matters of choice, others, the ones that matter most to them, are authentic, certain, truly "who we are."

For example, LGBTQ activists often take the view that sexual identities are genetically determined: people are "born that way."[3] Critical disability theorists and many disabled persons contend that what others see as "disabilities" are not burdens or contingencies but valuable, deeply constitutive features of their human personhood.[4] The Union for Reform Judaism's editor at large, Aron Hirt-Manheimer, has written that the belief of Jews that they possess a special identity as God's chosen people "is so deeply embedded in the Jewish psyche that it persists even among those who no longer believe in the faith of their ancestors. Paradoxically, while they would deny that Jews are any different from their gentile neighbors, they cannot bring themselves to totally abandon an idea that has defined Jewish existence since the Israelites encountered God at the foot of Mount Sinai."[5] Members of modern American indigenous tribes have adopted many different definitions of who is a "real Indian," but as the controversy over Elizabeth Warren's identity confirms, many fiercely insist that only their conception is valid.[6]

These minority groups are hardly alone in maintaining discourses and practices that appear to presume "essentialist" identities. The U.S. census famously (or infamously) gives American residents a set of choices for reporting their racial and ethnic identities, with the categories shaped by advocacy groups who argue strenuously for these categories' veracity even though they understand them in many different ways.[7] In recent times, perhaps no mainstream U.S. politician said "that is who we are as Americans" and "that is not who we are as Americans" more often than Barack Obama.[8] It is likely that he did this not in spite of his multiracial, multinational, multireligious origins, but precisely because they shaped his conception of what America should be.

Yet in much of the world today, it is conservative nationalist political movements and religious traditionalists who are insisting most often that they have core, essential identities that are being effaced and mistreated. In some cases, such as the Hindu nationalists of India, these movements represent popular majorities. In others, such as Protestant fundamentalists in the United States and anti-immigrant political parties in France, Germany, and elsewhere, they lack majoritarian approval at this writing. Nonetheless, it has become customary to call all these movements and views "populist." Many leaders of these populist groups contend that economic and cultural globalization, spurred on by political champions of demographic and cultural diversity, are eroding their people's capacities to be "who they are."

Consequently, they are mobilizing political support against many forms of globalization and diversity, as well as the actors and policies that they see advancing them. Even as they promise greater certainty and repose—partly *because* they promise greater certainty and repose—when they come to power, many of these populist movements enact harsh measures against all "others" whose identities they do not share. In so doing, leaders as diverse as Viktor Orbán in Hungary, Jair Bolsonaro in Brazil, and Xi Jinping in China have been quite explicit that, while they claim sovereign democratic authority from their "people," they have little if any regard for the values and practices of individual rights, civil liberties, and an independent judiciary that are defining features of modern liberal democracies. The rise of such leaders and movements to power in many lands, including a few that are in some ways faring better than many traditional liberal democracies, represents the most significant political development of the twenty-first century. Because these forms of populism threaten to confer legitimacy on authoritarian governance, they are also, after environmental catastrophe, the greatest global threat to human well-being today.

For that reason, the dangers posed by such populist movements and policies are my central concern in this book. I will first place the rise of (especially) right-wing, authoritarian forms of populism in the broader context of world developments that have fragmented older senses of community and membership. While not disputing now-standard accounts of the sources of modern populism, I focus here on "stories of peoplehood," which shine light on another less-discussed factor: the modern proliferation of rival stories about who we are in what leading analysts see as a new, complex, "nonpolar" world.[9] I will review examples of the modern fragmentation and multiplication of conflicting senses of political membership drawn from the three great waves of the construction of modern nation-states. They will include the post-Communist governments of the Czech Republic and Slovakia; the postimperial regimes of the United Arab Emirates and the Philippines; and dissident communities in two of the world's oldest nations, Northern Ireland in Great Britain and rural Wisconsin in the United States.

I will then consider the strategies and limitations of some leading responses to the more exclusionary and repressive forms of contemporary populism. I contend that, though every political leader and movement relies at least implicitly on some sort of story of their constituents' shared identity, many liberal and left-leaning leaders have been reluctant to oppose right-wing populist nationalist narratives with explicit countervailing stories of national identity. They fear, very reasonably, that nationalist accounts all too easily erode into narrow-minded, repressive chauvinism. Nonetheless, I will argue that authoritarian populisms should be met through the development of more positive, more egalitarian, and inclusive stories of national peoplehood. I will suggest the possibility for such stories in cases as different as Denmark, India, and Israel.

These arguments rest on two premises that some may resist. First is the belief that political contestation inevitably involves clashes between different narratives of political identities, policies, and purposes, among other elements. Second is the conviction that political outcomes are significantly shaped by whether these narratives are more or less resonant with their intended audiences, and whether they are more or less morally defensible. Against my view, many conceive of politics as driven chiefly by conflicting material interests and raw aspirations for power and domination, backed by coercive force. Narratives or stories are not thought to have much to do with it.

In my judgment, that view reveals the kind of failure to accept fully the partly constructed character of every human identity just noted. As scholars in a wide range of disciplines—including not only communications and cultural studies but also management and economics as well as political science—have come to recognize, our very notions of what our material interests are, what forms of power we should seek, and what our purposes are in deploying force all gain content from our conceptions of who we are and what we value.[10] In this spirit, Benedict Anderson influentially argued more than three decades ago that nations rest on shared imaginations of common identities.[11] Recently Yuval Harari has gone further, contending that *all* human communities depend on forms of "collective imagination" articulated in "shared myths" or stories.[12] In agreement, I will contend that the conceptions of material interests and desirable forms of power and force that play major roles in politics inevitably gain content from larger stories of our identities, even if some are more explicit and elaborate than others.

One sign that many have yet to absorb this reality is that analysts often treat "identity" politics as a distinctive subset of politics. If we recognize that all political groups are held together in part by stories of who they are, then we must acknowledge that all politics is identity politics. It is only a question of which identities we valorize. The politics of patriotism, of partisanship, of class conflicts, of clashing ideologies—indeed the cause of humanity in relation to the rest of existence—are all as much identity politics as are the politics of race, ethnicity, religion, gender, and sexuality. They all are carried on by groups and organizations, and within and between communities, whose senses of their interests and purposes are constructed in part through stories of who those groups, organizations, and communities are, and who their opponents are. Political contestation always includes conflicts among these stories of the participants' identities.

Consequently, throughout the world and throughout history, there has never been and never will be any escape from identity politics, or from the attendant need for stories of political peoplehood that are better rather than worse. Those most able to tell appealing stories of peoplehood for and within particular societies are, however, likely to be people who identify deeply with those societies. I believe it is their responsibility to help make those stories more politically effective and more morally defensible, insofar as they can. Consequently, here I will elaborate my arguments for constructive responses to narrowly nationalistic populisms most fully in regard to my own country, the United States of America. I will contend that President Donald Trump's "America First" vision of national peoplehood should be countered by more egalitarian, inclusive stories that draw on American traditions of democracy; the Constitution's quest for a more perfect union; and the project, set forth in the Declaration of Independence, of creating forms of government that can secure basic rights for all.

I hope those arguments will make clear that I do not seek to encourage people to evade or condemn the deep human longings for a secure sense of identity that shape most people's behavior. I share those longings. I seek here to help my fellow citizens of the United States, and my fellow members of the human species, to create and sustain through democratic engagement forms of political community that embody beneficial and fulfilling stories of shared identity. My scholarly work leads me to caution, however, that in this as in so many other regards, we can't always get all we want.

In particular, this book is not and cannot be a handbook on how to discover the true (and fortuitously progressive!) essences of our political identities that all should embrace, instead of xenophobic forms of nationalism. I believe it is time to accept fully both that all our identities are constituted in part by humanly crafted stories of who we are and who we should be *and* that the contents of those stories often involve none too veracious romantic elements. Frequently they include glorifying mythologies about the past and disgraceful erasures of ugly historical truths, even as they minimize or deny the reality that they are contingent human creations. Yet imperfect as all our stories are, we can find reasons to embrace some as the ones we wish to define ourselves by, and try to live by, in order to give our lives enjoyment and meaning. We can also strive to make our stories truer, wiser, and more beneficial over time.

One reason for optimism that we can find or craft worthy stories of ourselves is that we are shaped by many stories of who we might be, giving us some real choice about which of those stories to pursue and develop, which we choose to depart from. And though certainty is unlikely, I believe we are capable of making defensible and widely shared, if always contested and corrigible, judgments about which stories of ourselves are better, which are worse. Even if we cannot discover our "natural" or "essential" selves—certainly, we have not yet done so—we can reasonably decide for ourselves and with others what we think to be our better selves. We can then strive to become who we think we should be.

To do so, I will suggest, we must work harder at crafting good, if always imperfect, stories of political peoplehood that can engage with and compete with the populist stories, and the anxieties and resentments they articulate, that are driving politics in disturbing directions in many places today. Good stories must be ones that give voice to people's existing senses of aspects of themselves that they most value. They must also, however, express respect and a spirit of generosity toward others. These moral imperatives therefore often require people to question and change aspects of who they have been. Consequently, good stories of peoplehood will not enable people to say, "That is who we are!" with the secure faith in the worth of their "true" selves that many long for, and that many political leaders claim to provide. They will, however, enable people to say, "That is not who we want to be!" when they are confronted with dark portraits of themselves.

The danger will still remain that even in making that proclamation, leaders and citizens of political communities will advance narratives of their identities that deflect attention from bleak realities of their past and present misdeeds, in ways that perpetuate harms that they as a people have done.[13] Yet because it is difficult if not impossible for people to find value in lives without such narratives, it is difficult if not impossible to sustain a political movement or community through the travails that time always brings if they have no sustaining stories of identity and meaning. The best stories will include within them specifications of a wide range of policies, laws, and institutions that can respond to the most deeply felt needs and aspirations of community members; and they will include more. They will provide understandings of why those policies, laws, and institutions are appropriate for that people and their hopes and needs, why those measures can be expected to work, and why they can be deemed morally right. Here too, it is a mistake to think that we face a choice between pragmatically advancing concrete policies or poetically declaiming rhetorical stories. We can at most choose which we emphasize. All stories have policy implications, and even more, all policies derive their purposes from larger stories of the interests and values they serve. Sometimes, the values celebrated in those larger stories can set restraints on a people's misconduct.

Consequently, if leaders and citizens craft and win support for better rather than worse political narratives, those narratives can enable people to say, "This is who we wish to be, who we choose to be: one people, and a people that seeks to overcome our failings, to be better and to do better by all whom we have affected and are affecting, beginning with ourselves." That outcome is not a formula for sure political or policy success. Efforts to articulate, build support for, and live by always-contested, always evolving stories of "who we are and who we should be" can always fail. Even when the proponents of such stories gain victories, they cannot realistically hope to end all uncertainty, answer all doubts, and guarantee a secure and fulfilling political future for themselves and their communities. Repose is not our destiny. It is unlikely, however, that we can progress far toward any of those goals unless we develop stories of political identity that can energize and guide all who seek to place politics on better paths than those we find ourselves stumbling upon today.

1
A Cacophony of Stories

The New Populist Moment

As the second decade of the twenty-first century approaches its end, the increasing prominence and power of movements and leaders labeled "populist" is the most striking feature of politics around the world. Journalists and scholars alike most often apply the term to anti-immigrant, authoritarian-leaning leaders and parties like Viktor Orbán and Fidesz in Hungary; Geert Wilders and the Party for Freedom in the Netherlands; the National Front (rechristened the National Rally) in France; the Law and Justice Party in Poland; the Danish People's Party; the AfD in Germany; Jair Bolsonaro in Brazil; and many others. Analysts also often use the term "populist" to describe nationalist authoritarian leaders like Rodrigo Duterte in the Philippines and sometimes Vladimir Putin in Russia and Xi Jinping in China. Some especially apply it to figures emphasizing religious conceptions of national identity, like Recep Tayyip Erdoğan and the Justice and Development Party in Turkey and Narendra Modi and the BJP in India.

But "populist" is applied as well to more secular, economically left-leaning actors like Hugo Chávez and his successor

Nicolás Maduro in Venezuela, Alexis Tsipras and Syriza in Greece, the Shinawatra siblings in Thailand, and Bernie Sanders in the United States. Many proponents of Brexit, such as Britain's new Prime Minister Boris Johnson, proudly claim the title. The current U.S. President, Donald J. Trump, calls himself a "nationalist," but he makes it clear that he sees himself as the champion of the "people" against a corrupt "Washington establishment." Unlike Trump, not all of these populist leaders and movements are now in power, and there is no guarantee that any particular populist leader will stay in power for long. But they already hold many offices in many nations; they are gaining support in many others; and as a result, they are shaping political developments everywhere.

Given the variety of leaders and movements being called populist, analysts have devoted a great deal of attention to two questions: first, how to define populism, and second, how to explain its explosive growth globally—with answers to the second question partly turning on answers to the first. Scholars have paid somewhat less attention to the question I focus on in this book: what types of responses to pathological forms of populism are feasible and desirable? Because I believe beneficial stories of peoplehood are necessary—though not sufficient—to combat the worst forms of populism today, I will offer an account in the next chapter of what the elements of such stories are. To help readers judge that account, here I review briefly the current scholarship on what we should call populism, and what its causes may be. I will argue that attention to the political roles of stories can add fresh answers to both of those questions.

DEFINITIONS AND DIAGNOSES

In recent public discourse, perhaps the most influential account of populism is Jan-Werner Müller's in his appropriately entitled book *What Is Populism?* Müller argues that at its core, populism is a moralized antipluralism, an inherently illiberal form of identity politics that is given to internal authoritarianism and allegiance to a leader believed to embody popular will.[1] He rejects calling such populism "pathological" because he believes the label "pathology" implies that supporters of populist leaders are irrational, with few reasonable grievances or goals.[2] He acknowledges, however, that his definition is most descriptive of the contemporary populist movements in his native Europe. It does not work well for most of the pre-Trump examples of populism in America, particularly the late-nineteenth-century People's Party.[3] That party and other American farm-labor populist movements of that era were largely internally democratic. More than most organizations in their day, they embraced racial and ethnic minorities and women as equals, generally only rhetorically, but sometimes as leaders. They also did not follow an authoritarian figure. When the Populists embraced William Jennings Bryan as their messianic candidate in 1896, they may have unwisely suspended some critical judgments, but they did not abandon their democratic commitments. Nor did Bryan himself, whatever his other shortcomings.[4]

I am inclined to say, against Müller, that our conception of populism should be broad enough to include the American People's Party as well as other self-proclaimed populist movements that are broadly democratic. In general, it is both respectful to call groups by the names they wished to be called and important not to become so focused on our own academic typologies that we lose sight of how words are being used in the broader world. It is not wrong, however, to attach to groups' preferred descriptions the modifiers that we see as appropriate. Consequently, unlike Müller, I choose to apply the term "pathological populisms" to strongly antipluralist, illiberal, and authoritarian movements that present themselves as populist. I do so not because I see their adherents as irrational, but because they are the variants of populism that are most likely to produce the ill effects with which Müller, I, and many others are concerned. They are the ones most likely to exclude, repress, and persecute ethnic and religious others and to retain the mere forms of constitutional self-governance while actually imposing dictatorships.

Many other scholars writing on populism also adopt more expansive definitions than Müller's. Perhaps the most influential in academic circles is Cas Mudde, often writing with Cristóbal Kaltwasser. They have long argued for what they term a "minimal definition" of populism as a "thin-centred ideology," one lacking elaborate content, "that considers society to be ultimately separated into two homogeneous and antagonistic camps, the 'pure people' versus the 'corrupt elite,' and which argues that politics should be an expression of the volonté générale (general will) of the people."[5] For these authors, populist movements can be internally democratic, without subservience to a leader claiming to embody that people's general will, though such leaders often arise.

Others argue that even this minimal definition goes a bit too far. They contend that "the people" in populist movements need not be conceived as homogeneous, pure, or possessing a Rousseauian "general will." Many scholars, building on Ernesto Laclau, maintain that to be considered populist, a view or movement need only insist, first, that politics is fundamentally about clashes between the people and the elite, however defined; and second, that only the people can confer legitimacy on political and governmental actions.[6] Many contributors to the recent *Oxford Handbook of Populism* are still more parsimonious. They see populism simply as *"a thin-centered ideology that posits a struggle between the will of the common people and a conspiring elite."*[7] This minimalist definition allows us to deem "populist" movements with both left-leaning and right-leaning economic agendas, as well as more centrist ones. Venezuelan socialists, Danish social welfare state advocates, pro-market British Tories, and Trumpian economic nationalists can all be included. The *Oxford Handbook* definition also enables us to let in internally democratic parties and movements that have embraced a significant degree of pluralism and that have not followed an authoritarian leader, like the American People's Party. To conform to both common and academic usages as fully as possible, I will use the *Handbook*'s minimalist, expansive, and inclusive definition of populism here—but with one important addition, derived from my focus on stories of peoplehood, that I will specify shortly.

First, I must acknowledge that choosing this broad definition makes responding to the second question, the causes of the contemporary surge in populist movements, even more challenging. The diverse streams of populism flowing today are not likely all to trace to the same spring. I will not attempt to work out all those differences here, however, because analysts of modern populism are actually fairly united on the basic factors they discuss. They disagree, sometimes sharply, on those factors' relative weight. But my argument will be that good stories of peoplehood should include responses to all the concerns that populists are expressing, giving greatest weight to those that are most pronounced in their settings.

What do scholars see as the sources of populism? Some emphasize *economic* worries as modern populism's deepest roots—including insecurities prompted by heightening inequalities and many dimensions of economic globalization, as well as technological innovations. These economic anxieties are often reinforced by perceptions that mainstream political parties and leaders don't care about poorer people's economic woes, or worse, are corrupt tools of wealthy elites. Other analysts stress *cultural* factors—a sense of lost status and secure identity in the face of demographic and cultural shifts wrought by immigration, secularization, minority liberation movements, and other trends.[8] These scholars see populist adherents as enraged at cosmopolitan cultural elites, who they feel to be contemptuous of traditionalist beliefs and ways of life. Some writers go further and portray most contemporary populists as driven not just by cultural traditionalism but by virulent racial and religious bigotry.

In a 2017 essay on the causes of populism, Kirk Hawkins, Madeleine Read, and Teun Pauwels see force in both economic and cultural explanations. They also call, however, for greater attention to the "content of populist ideas," the reasons people have for deciding that conspiring elites, whether economic or cultural or both, are ruining their ways of life.[9] These scholars see populism as rooted in faith in democracy, accompanied by convictions that if things seem bad, leaders must be failing the people. Consequently, individuals become receptive to appeals targeting elites for blame.

I too see great power in both the economic and cultural explanations for contemporary populisms. I will not focus on those causes here or seek to determine their relative weight, because I do not wish to challenge prevailing accounts, only to add to them. I will build on the argument that we should attend to the content of populist ideas and that most populist supporters genuinely embrace the central conception of democracy, that the people, rightly defined, are the source of political legitimacy. However, I wish to take this concern with populist ideas in a different direction from what most analysts are pursuing. Hawkins, Read, and Pauwels, for example, call for more attention to the voters' policy attitudes, in the manner of mainstream public opinion scholars. They do not examine who different populist movements define as "the people" whose will and interests should govern, and why those "people," and not others, deserve to govern. Unlike populist leaders and media voices, they do not give much attention to populist versions of stories of peoplehood.

Yet even though globalizing forces creating job displacements, economic inequalities, demographic diversity, heightened urbanization, and often senses of disempowerment provide conditions conducive to populist revolts against established elites, those revolts are neither inevitable nor wholly self-generated. It is vital to recognize that there are always elements of political agency at work. Leaders—who may include public intellectuals, artists, prominent civil society figures, and movement activists—must advance populist stories of peoplehood that persuade people to interpret their experiences in certain ways. Failure to attend to populist stories of who the people are, how they are aggrieved, and what they should do can lead scholars to overlook both a significant contributing cause and a possible cure for pathological populisms.

That is why I wish to add one element to the *Oxford Handbook of Populism*'s minimalist definition of populism. Scholars and political participants must recognize that each populist ideology includes a story (or, more often, overlapping stories) about who the people are and why they are endangered by the policies supported by corrupt or at least unpatriotic elites. Viktor Orbán valorizes the distinctive character of "the romantic Hungarians" and "Hungarian genius" while insisting that "there is no cultural identity in a population without a stable ethnic population," so that Hungary has to be "defended against the migrant flow and invasion" favored by the "transnational elite."[10] Recep Erdoğan's oft-stated views on the character of the Turkish people have been criticized as "assertively Muslim" and "skeptical of other nations and global elites," though he and his supporters contend that he is even more true than Turkey's modern founder, Atatürk, to the Turkish people's historical identity as a world-leading nation that can accommodate multiple communities within it.[11] Boris Johnson has proclaimed that Britain is the world's "soft power superpower" because of its economy and culture, as well as its "charm and eccentricity," even as he has also asserted that in modern times it has become a virtual "colony" ruled by the European Union's bureaucrats.[12] We will see many similar examples in the pages to come, and many more could be added. If we hope to render populist movements more genuinely democratic and respectful of the rights and dignity of all, we must engage with the identities, values, and concerns expressed in these populist stories, offering narratives that respond to them credibly, while also supporting broadly beneficial policies.

TURNING TO STORIES

Even readers convinced that human interests and drives are not simply self-interpreting may at this point still ask: why must political leaders elaborate not just narratives of human values, goals, and strategies for realizing them, but stories of political peoplehood, defining what they hope their audiences will accept as the best account of the identities of their particular political societies? One answer prominent in recent political theories is the recognition that all modern democracies confront what scholars call the "boundary problem."[13] This is the foundational question of who should be counted as a member of a self-governing people, a *demos.* Although in democracies the demos is supposed to have sovereign authority to decide all major questions, in regard to this issue, that standard of legitimacy is little help. We cannot appeal to the demos to decide who belongs to the demos, since doing so presupposes the answer to the question we are trying to get answered.

Many writers, including me, have argued that issues of who belongs are best worked out over time through political processes within and across the existing structure of societies that are as inclusive and egalitarian as proves politically feasible, with the aim of creating political communities that are both more expansive and more democratic over time.[14] Yet whether or not political actors accept that goal, whenever they seek to answer the "boundary problem," they cannot avoid advancing accounts of who should constitute "the people," who should not, and why. Consequently, not only in modern democratic theories but in all modern political societies espousing popular sovereignty, the boundary problem creates a virtually unavoidable imperative for political participants to put forth stories of peoplehood.[15]

On its face, this argument applies only to modern democratic regimes, or at least societies claiming to regard their people as sovereign. But in his best-selling book *Sapiens,* the Israeli historian Yuval Harari provides a further and yet more sweeping explanation for the prevalence of such narratives. He argues that *all* large-scale forms of human cooperation—"whether a modern state, a medieval church, an ancient city or an archaic tribe"—are "rooted in . . . people's collective imagination," in the "stories" that they tell one another.[16] Harari believes that the distinguishing feature of our species, *Homo sapiens*—the deepest source of its ability to "rule the world"—is our capacity to "cooperate flexibly in large numbers." He thinks that large-scale cooperation, in turn, rests on our abilities to compose and embrace "myths" or "stories" of our shared identities, interests, and purposes.[17] It is belief in these stories that persuades us to trust one another, and to feel that "it would be worthwhile to help one another."[18]

I am not bold enough to proclaim with Harari's assurance that our storytelling and story-believing abilities are what set us Homo sapiens apart from, and above, all other species on earth, enabling our distant ancestors to conquer mastodons and

Neanderthals. I am confident, however, that the politics of Homo sapiens, including both our achievements in forming and sustaining political communities and our conflicts within and between them, have always depended on those abilities. I have long contended that political communities are always created and sustained by combinations of coercive force and persuasive stories. To be sure, as Max Weber knew, it is the element of coercive force that most distinguishes political communities from many other sorts of human associations, some sustained by stories alone. It is a mistake, however, to think that political communities rest fundamentally on force and not stories. In Harari's words, one cannot "organize an army solely by coercion." There must be "some true believers" in the army's ranks if it is to be relied upon in conflicts.[19]

I have argued that stories of peoplehood work to inspire such true belief, among soldiers and citizens alike. They do so by fostering senses of trust among members of a community, and between the members and their leaders, as well as senses of the worth of their membership in that community.[20] I have further defined "political peoples" as not only built by both force and stories, but also as those "human associations, groups, and communities that are commonly understood to assert that their members owe them a measure of allegiance against the demands of other associations, communities, and groups." It is these calls for allegiance that foster the forms of both conflict and cooperation that politics involves. Consequently, "the more demanding the claims, the more political the group."[21] This definition also means that there is a wide range of weaker and stronger forms of political peoplehood.

I have further maintained that for any story of political peoplehood to sustain senses of collective identity and cooperative endeavors over time, it must persuasively advance three basic themes, with suitable accompanying policies. Though stories often contain different emphases and achieve different degrees of success, each story must have an economic theme, with policies promising both personal and collective material well-being. It must have a political power theme, and policies promising both personal safety and community power sufficient for collective self-defense, if not expansion. Often these themes also promise a measure of political voice. Finally, it must have a constitutive theme, again expressed in appropriate policies.

A constitutive theme presents "membership in a particular people as intrinsic to who the members really are, because of traits deemed to be normatively good."[22] One of my core claims is that, though no political society can endure if its governors do not offer credible economic and political power themes and policies that generate confirming results for a critical mass of its members, no society can long maintain itself through economic and power benefits alone. There will inevitably be down times. So a political community must also be sustained by senses of allegiance rooted in beliefs that belonging to the community is part of its members' core identities, and a part that gives their lives meaning and worth. Constitutive themes may feature religion, ancestry, ethnicity, race, gender roles, language, culture, class, customs, history, and more. But they always present the traits they feature as having high value, and as integral to "who we are."

Joining Meral Ugur Cinar, I have also argued that narratives of political identity have certain types of formal structures, and that they work best when their structures and content themes are well matched. For stories of political peoplehood, three types of structures are most prevalent, sometimes found in combination. The first type is the mechanistic narrative, which portrays political societies as governed by unchanging laws or regularities of behavior that generate predictable patterns—often cycles—in their lives over time. The second type is a teleological organicist form of narrative, which portrays political societies as on paths of growth and development that may fluctuate, but that tend in the long run to move societies toward an ultimate end state. The third type is the contextual account, which maps how the interactions of different units in societies foster change in those units and in the society as a whole, in ways that are comprehensible but that do not work toward any specific telos, or display unfaltering lawlike behavioral regularities.[23]

Despite their different contents, we will see that the formal structure of most populist narratives is mechanistic. The governing law that explains political developments is: "When the people are in power, all is well; when elites take over, all goes to ruin." This structure is well suited to advance themes of the need to solve all current problems by returning power to the people—or their populist leaders. The narratives of such leaders depict a dramatic cycle in which, in happier times, the people once had power; then they lost power to corrupt elites, and everything deteriorated; but if they regain power, they and their political community will be great again. Although populist stories usually convey economic grievances and concerns about both personal physical safety and national security, along with remedial proposals, generally these narratives rely most heavily on constitutive themes to answer the core question of who the people are that deserve to be sovereign. They invoke a shared culture, religion, ethnicity, ideology, history, or other valued features of identity to delineate why the people are great, who should be counted as members—and who should be counted out.

Because constitutive themes so often play this crucial role, my previous discussions of stories of peoplehood have focused on them, even though they are not stressed in contemporary political science as much as economic and power interests. I have also emphasized nationalist narratives, or "stories of nationhood," because they remain the most prevalent and demanding stories of political peoplehood, the ones most likely to effectively claim supreme authority today. To understand fully the appeal of contemporary nationalist movements, however, we must take note of the empirical evidence indicating that, though the primacy of nation-states has not yet been overthrown in the global political order, it has been eroding for some time. As a result, intertwined with the economic and cultural concerns that many scholars of populism have detailed is an additional but less widely recognized contributing factor to the rise of modern populisms, particularly nationalistic populisms.

This factor is the decline in recent decades of stories of political peoplehood that are genuinely hegemonic, and the corresponding proliferation of thematically varied and conflicting stories, some highlighting economic benefits, some political power concerns, others a wide range of constitutive themes. Though many of these stories are nationalistic, many others are stridently antinationalist, championing a great diversity of possible memberships and allegiances, both transnational and subnational. Some of the stories put forth by nonnational groups and communities are highly demanding, others less so; but many do press people to heed them, and not their national governments or other putative authorities, in many conflicts. In aggregate, the burgeoning of these multiple types of political peoples has produced a cacophony of clashing stories of identities and obligations that many find painful. In this turbulent environment, millions if not billions of people are once again finding themselves attracted to the simple, familiar siren songs of populist nationalisms.

A PLETHORA OF PEOPLES

Until recently, many analysts stressed that globalization was bringing about greater economic, ideological, and cultural homogeneity—making the world "flat," in Thomas Friedman's famous phrase. In some regards, particularly economic policies after the fall of communism, there is no doubt that significant convergence on broadly similar approaches occurred in recent decades.[24] But nationalist populists like Donald Trump are now challenging even some of these developments, particularly free trade agreements. More broadly, today many perceive a "dialectic of globalisation and fragmentation" at work, with heightened communications and transportation systems and expanded economic, social, and political networks facilitating the growth of many diverse communities, within and beyond the boundaries of existing nations, even as other differences are diminishing.[25]

In so doing, globalization and fragmentation have fostered a mushrooming of highly varied stories of peoplehood that is in many ways exciting and promising. But many people still find it deeply unsettling—because it is. It is both a consequence of, and a contributing factor to, the ways contemporary projects of state building and state maintaining are faltering in many regions, leading to estimates that up to 80 percent of the world's people reside in limited or failed states.[26] When people feel that their nation-states are not doing well, and when they find alternate communities that appear to promise more and better, the stage is set for heightened embrace of rival stories of political peoplehood that challenge the dominance of narratives of national identity. But these conditions also provide motives and opportunities for proponents of nationalistic narratives to push back.

I do not wish to overstate the novelty of the present. For as far back as we know, human beings have always had what we now term multiple identities—as bearers of certain genders, as family members, as adherents of religious communities, as practitioners of occupations, as participants in political societies, and more. Still, it is likely that through most of human history, few people felt routinely confronted, as many are now, by so many diverse and conflicting stories of what their core political peoplehood should be. Though our story-creating abilities have enabled people for millennia to imagine societies and ways of life very different from their own, some important things really have changed. Modern communications systems, greater mobility, and urbanizing trends have shifted more and more of the world's population into extraordinarily diverse and extensively wired global cities, making exposure to multiple stories almost inescapable.

In contrast, most people throughout most of human history lived in relative isolation. As shown in Figure 1.1, up through the end of World War II, more than two-thirds of the world's population lived in rural areas, with limited access to mass communications systems. All their lives, they mostly heard long-familiar stories of who they were and might be, told by local familial, religious, and political leaders. Even if there were higher political figures and broader communities that claimed authority over them, those authorities generally seemed remote. Stories depicting identities and ways of life substantially different from their own seemed more like entertaining fantasies than concrete options.

The stories they heard, moreover, generally presented their multiple identities as mutually compatible, and at any rate as largely unalterable. People's familial statuses, gender roles, occupations, religious memberships, and political allegiances were all interwoven into relatively coherent senses of who they were and what they should be—views that most of those around them shared and reinforced. Few experienced frequent demands to reconsider their political identities and obligations, nor did they have many tangible opportunities to do so. Consequently, scholars of nationalism including Benedict Anderson, Ernest Gellner, and Francis Fukuyama have concluded, in Fukuyama's

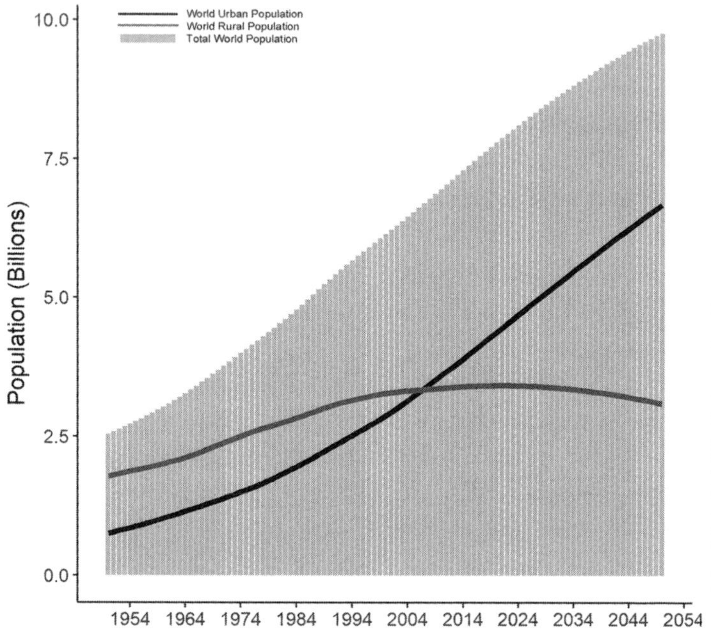

Figure 1.1. From rural to urban. Source: Created by Zachary Koslowski with data acquired from United Nations, Department of Economic and Social Affairs, Population Division. "World Urbanization Prospects: The 2018 Revision," https://www.un.org/development/desa/publications/2018-revision-of-world-urbanization-prospects.html.

words, that identity did "not really exist as a problem in premodern societies." Though there was "a differentiation of social identities," the limits on mobility meant that people "did not have much choice" in their associations. Consequently, it is likely that few spent "a lot of time sitting around asking themselves, 'Who am I, really?' "[27]

None of this means that "premodern" life was generally pastoral and peaceful. Conflicts and power struggles have been endemic throughout history. However, these conflicts generally arose from people seeking to heighten their importance, or gain a higher station, among the conventional roles and statuses defined by the prevailing narratives of their communities. Army commanders wanted to be emperors. Barons wanted to be kings. Low priests wanted to be high priests. Third wives wanted to be first wives. But people rarely faced internal conflicts over which political community they should call their own, or what their core identity should be.

Political societies often did compete with other societies, with the disputes frequently settled by force. Conquerors often imposed on the conquered a new political identity, expressed in the victors' stories of peoplehood. Still, until roughly the past four hundred years, most human beings either were part of empires or lived in villages, small cities, or nomadic tribes that managed to maintain or to regain their autonomy.

Mostly, they were part of empires. Until the era of decolonization that followed World War II, the bulk of the world's territory was governed by imperial regimes of one sort or another—from the Assyrian empire to the Persian to the sequence of Chinese empires, as well as the Arab Caliphate, the Roman, Byzantine, Ottoman, Mughal, Incan, and Aztec empires, the Spanish, French, and British empires, and many more (Figure 1.2).[28]

Yet the imperially governed were often loosely governed. Although these empires varied enormously, most had multilevel, overlapping jurisdictions, and, apart from collecting taxes and compelling military service, most shared power with the local leaders they favored in the communities they conquered. They permitted considerable local self-governance that left unchallenged a wide array of religions, occupations, ethnic identities, and cultural ways of life, and thus a great variety of traditional identities, even as direct resistance to imperial rule met brutal punishments.[29] Though they propagated stories of

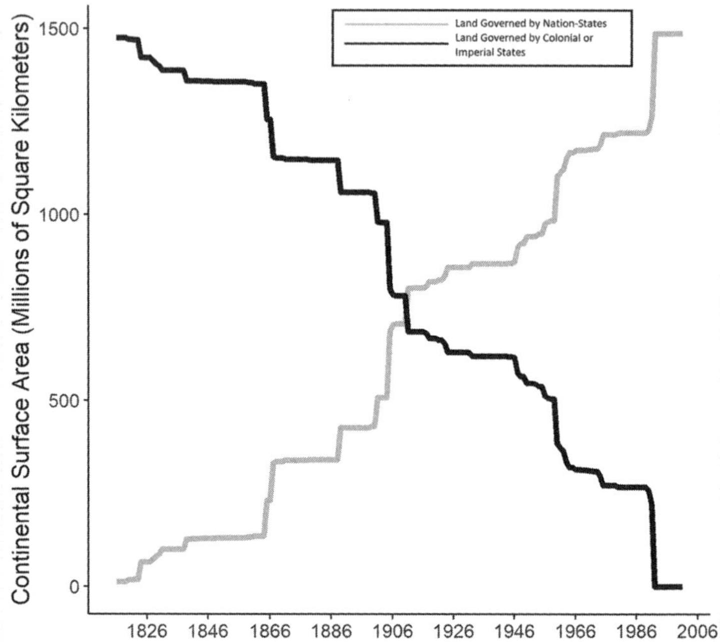

Figure 1.2. From empires to nation-states. Source: Created by Zachary Koslowski using data from http://www.columbia.edu/~aw2951/Datasets.html, the basis for a similar graph in Andreas Wimmer, Lars-Erik Cederman, and Brian Min, "Ethnic Politics and Armed Conflict: A Configurational Analysis of a New Global Dataset," *American Sociological Review* 74, no. 2 (2009): 316–337.

imperial peoplehood that shaped the identities of those they governed, for many subjects, their imperial political identity was a relatively unobtrusive layer added on to the familiar ones that continued to characterize who they were and what they did on most days of their lives. Even those who fought against their imperial conquerors generally did so out of a firm sense of their preceding, traditional identities and obligations that let them see their political world as a straightforward "us" versus "them."

Then came the global decolonization movements that followed World War II. The long period when empires were the most prevalent form of political regime around the globe gave way to a new era that we often think of as older than it really is. This is the era in which national states became the overwhelmingly predominant kind of political society worldwide, culminating a process that began in Europe in, at the earliest, the sixteenth century and gained ideological impetus in the late eighteenth century with the American and French Revolutions.[30] Though exact numbers vary with different definitions, the world possessed roughly 50 sovereign states in 1945. By 1989, as the end of the European and Japanese empires in Africa and Asia generated a host of new national states, the number had more than tripled, to more than 180.[31] For the first time, national states governed most of the world's population (Figure 1.3).

This multiplication of states did not, however, foster senses of fragmented and competing political identities to the degree that many are experiencing today, for one major reason. This brave new world of national states existed within an overarching, hegemonic structure, driven by the rivalry between the capitalist United States and its global allies and the Communist Soviet Union and its allies. Many states, to be sure, were unaligned, and most states experienced some level of internal contestation over how they should align themselves, especially those wrestling with the legacies of imperialism, which included many forms of continuing imperial influence. Even so, during the Cold War, most people's conceptions of their political identities gained some simplicity and clarity from their answer to one great question: "On which side of the Iron Curtain do we stand? With the communists or with the capitalists?" The centrality of this divide helped states in both camps to accept new transnational agreements and institutions, including NATO on the one hand and the Warsaw Pact on the other,

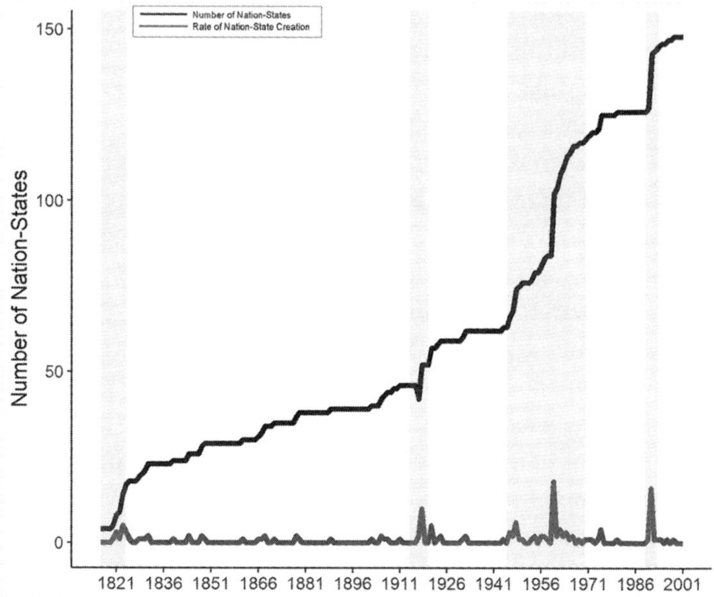

Figure 1.3. Rise in number of nation-states. Created by Zachary Koslowski using data from http://www.columbia.edu/~aw2951/Datasets.html, compiled for Andreas Wimmer, Lars-Erik Cederman, and Brian Min, "Ethnic Politics and Armed Conflict: A Configurational Analysis of a New Global Dataset," *American Sociological Review* 74, no. 2 (2009): 316–337.

which they might otherwise have seen as reducing their national sovereignty. It also prompted much of the West to support new pro-capitalist global economic institutions, including the International Monetary Fund, the World Bank, and, eventually, the World Trade Organization, even as Communist nations like Cuba and North Korea relied on aid from the Soviet Union and the People's Republic of China.

I grew up in this world, and I can attest that it made choices about political identity, not just for states but for individuals, seem more straightforward than they do today. The threat of nuclear war was always in the back and often in the front of our minds, swallowing up all other differences and concerns and promoting relatively integrated senses of who we were. When in 1961 John F. Kennedy structured his inaugural address around the opposition between "two great and powerful groups of nations . . . both racing to alter that uncertain balance of terror that stays the hand of mankind's final war," he told a compelling story of global politics in which we all knew our place.[32]

Then in 1989, the Cold War ended. The Berlin Wall came down and Communist regimes in Eastern Europe began to collapse, with the Soviet Union itself falling two years later. The demise of communism launched another wave of postimperial state building, so that today the United Nations has 195 member states. As this wave began, Francis Fukuyama stirred a global debate by asking whether the eclipse of the world's major ideological alternative to capitalism and liberal democracy meant "the end of history."[33] For a time, the answer appeared to be yes. The United States stood as the world's sole hegemon, with its economic and political systems providing the models to be imitated by all the nations of the world.

But within two decades, the president of the Council on Foreign Relations, Richard Haass, declared that although the "unipolar moment" of U.S. dominance had been "real," it was already coming to an end, making it only "a moment" in historical terms.[34] Haass argued that this transient unipolarity was giving way not to a newly bipolar or multipolar world but to an "age of nonpolarity." He contended that in contrast to "classic multipolarity," there were now "many more power centers, and quite a few of these poles are not nation-states. Indeed, one of the cardinal features of the contemporary international system is that nation-states have lost their monopoly on power and in some domains their preeminence as well. States are being challenged from above, by regional and global organizations; from below, by militias; and from the side, by a variety of nongovernmental organizations (NGOs) and corporations. Power is now found in many hands and in many places."[35]

As examples of these many hands, Haass pointed not only to the nations that were powers in particular regions of the world, like Brazil, Nigeria, South Korea, and Australia. He also listed global organizations like the International Monetary Fund, the United Nations, and the World Bank; regional bodies like the European Union, the African Union, and the Organization of American States; transnational bodies with more specific missions like the International Energy Agency, OPEC, and the World Health Organization; powerful sub-national states like California and Uttar Pradesh; global cities like New York and Shanghai; multinational corporations; global media outlets like al Jazeera and CNN; militia like Hezbollah and the Taliban; and "political parties, religious institutions and movements, terrorist organizations (al Qaeda), drug cartels, and NGOs of a more benign sort (the Bill and Melinda Gates Foundation, Doctors Without Borders, Greenpeace)."[36]

If anything, Haass understated the developments contributing to nonpolarity. He did not call attention to the movements for regional autonomy or outright secession, as in Quebec, Scotland, Catalonia, Chechnya, and many other areas, which have posed severe challenges to long-established nation-states in recent decades. He also did not document the spectacular growth of international NGOs, which has added thousands of actors to the global scene (Figure 1.4).

Most pertinently for my arguments here, Haass also did not note that every one of the entities he listed sustains itself in part through organizational stories that present its mission, and so its membership, as enormously valuable. In some instances,

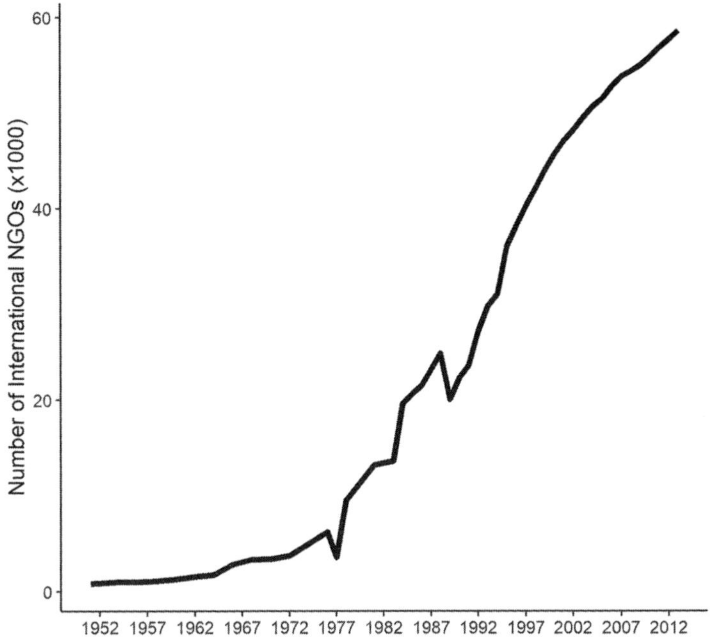

Figure 1.4. Rise in number of international NGOs. Source: Created by Zachary Koslowski from Union of International Associations, "Historical Overview of Number of International Organizations by Type," https://uia.org/sites/uia.org/files/misc_pdfs/stats/Historical_overview_of_number_of_international_organizations_by_type_1909-2013.pdf.

though certainly not all, the memberships are held out as morally obligatory, even when they are in conflict with national duties. The European Union claims certain kinds of formal authority over its member nations. The Taliban portrays the commitments of Muslims to follow the religious laws it enforces as more fundamental than whatever they may owe to Pakistan or Afghanistan (which the Taliban asserts the authority to lead). Greenpeace, which began when activists placed themselves in the way of nuclear testing, professes to engage only in "nonviolent confrontation," but many of its members and other environmentalists clearly regard their moral mission to save the planet as exceeding their allegiances to any national government.[37] In a world that is indeed now best described as nonpolar, all these groups and many more constitute competing political peoples. They have created a clamorous chorus of conflicting calls to pledge allegiance to them.

Modern Sites of Contesting Stories

Although most states today are confronting challenges from these rising numbers of alternative accounts of their would-be constituents' possible political memberships and obligations, the specific character of those challenges differs in every case. There are nonetheless some commonalities. The nations formed out of the most recent wave of new nation building following the fall of communism have been particularly embroiled in questions of whether they should emphasize new embraces of principles of liberal democracy, or forms of ethnonationalism. The nations that emerged from the breaking up of Western empires often face struggles to define their appropriate boundaries, as well as their appropriate relationships with their former imperial governors. The "original" nation-states of Europe and North America face the discontents of both minority communities that may never have wanted to be part of those nations in the first place and traditionally dominant groups who fear they are losing their places. In the remainder of this chapter I examine examples of each of these categories, considering the Czech Republic and Slovakia; the United Arab Emirates and the Philippines; and dissident identities within Great Britain, the Ulster-Scots of Northern Ireland, and in the United States, the rural citizens of Wisconsin.

THE CZECH REPUBLIC AND SLOVAKIA

Like residents in many other parts of past empires, the citizens of the former Soviet satellite nations have often found it difficult to construct coherent, much less compelling, stories of peoplehood to replace the ones shaped by having long stood for or against an imperial regime, or in these cases, for or against the communist or capitalist bloc. Complicating their task is the sometimes overlooked reality that through 1989, many Soviet bloc states, such as Yugoslavia, Czechoslovakia, and the Soviet Union itself, structured themselves not only as Communist regimes but also as ethnofederal states, with subdivisions and even personal identity cards that drew on and reinforced preexisting ethnocultural communities. They did so in part to elicit support for their political regimes beyond what the economic and political power themes of communist ideologies could summon. Since communism's fall, these states have faced choices about whether they should remain unitary or divide, perhaps along regional or ethnic lines. They have also had to decide what kinds of national identities they or their successor states should embrace. They have responded in different ways.

In 1990, the former Czechoslovak Socialist Republic became the Czech and Slovak Federative Republic, and then in 1992 it broke into two new states, the Czech and Slovak Republics, the latter commonly called Slovakia. As Nadya Nedelsky has shown, the Czech Republic, like most of the former Soviet bloc states in the 1990s, adopted what is frequently termed a civic conception of its identity, stressing that the state was a federation of free and equal citizens, dedicated to human rights and democracy. The Slovak Republic chose instead to conceive of its identity in ethnic terms. Its constitution identified itself as the product of the "Slovak Nation," exercising the "natural right of nations to self-determination" in order to advance "the political and cultural heritage of our forefathers," while also allowing a place for "minority nationalities" within its territory.[38]

Both republics, however, included some residents who still identified primarily as Communists. Others remained loyal to the formerly united Czechoslovakia. Still others were more strongly attached to the kind of political identity proclaimed in the republic where they did not reside than to that proclaimed in the one in which they did. Many more were simply uncertain about who or what their political identities should be. In each of the new republics, moreover, national minorities worried that their new states would not adequately protect them against discrimination, or recognize their distinctive identities.[39] The members of both these new states thus faced multiple competing stories of their political peoplehood that were no longer subordinated to their membership in the Soviet bloc.

Many other formerly communist nations have faced the same issues. Some, like Hungary and Poland, have swung between more civic and more ethnic national self-conceptions. Others, like Russia itself, have faced internal separatist movements. In most of these countries, nationalist populists have been or have recently become a rising force, especially when their populations have confronted economic stresses and heightened immigration pressures. In 2017 the Czech Republic elected as prime minister a wealthy former Communist, Andrej Babiš, who has reinvented himself as an anti-immigrant nationalist, assailing "multiculturalism" and insisting that Czechs have to "fight for what our ancestors built here."[40] Slovakia has held fast to a strongly ethnic conception of its national identity and remained highly homogeneous, despite a slight uptick in immigrants after it joined the European Union.[41] It even more steadfastly opposes accepting migrants and refugees, particularly non-Christians.[42]

THE UNITED ARAB EMIRATES

Many new nations created by earlier decolonization movements in the Middle East, Africa, and Asia confront somewhat different challenges in constructing and sustaining allegiance-inspiring national identities. Frequently, these former colonies have boundaries drawn by their imperial governors, who created "communities" that did not reflect deep historical formations and were not chosen by their indigenous residents. To take one striking example: although the Arab sheikhdoms that now form part of the United Arab Emirates were never formally colonies of the British empire, Great Britain long used treaties with its preferred sheikhs to exercise control over the region, especially after the discovery of oil in Bahrain in 1932.[43] In 1968, however, the British chose to withdraw from the Persian Gulf, initiating discussions among the British-protected Gulf states that led in 1971 to the founding of the United Arab Emirates. As Calvert Jones has detailed, this new political regime has since its inception faced major difficulties in fostering a common national identity among its members. There simply was no historical UAE identity on which to build, not even a sense of common cause born of shared anticolonial struggles. Most UAE residents instead grew up with strong, distinct, and often conflicting tribal identities.

The UAE did have oil money, however, as well as inherited tribal customs in which rulers provided goods to their tribesmen. It is therefore not surprising that early on, the UAE government sought to foster loyalty through an economics-centered story of peoplehood with an enticing teleological structure. They told those they governed, in effect, "If you embrace membership in the UAE, you will be eligible for state-provided benefits in the form of 'land, water, houses, clothing, shoes, food, hospitals, vehicles,' " and more.[44] Purchasing national loyalty primarily through the provision of material goods, however, is a problematic strategy. It tends to produce innumerable claimants for membership, requiring sharp constraints on access to citizenship if citizens are indeed to receive extensive material benefits. It can also easily foster a "rentier mentality," an ethos of self-indulgent, lazy dependency.

By the 1990s, according to Jones, UAE rulers had become vividly conscious of these problems. They also knew that reliance on oil could not last forever and that they would need new strategies to maintain economic success in a world increasingly dominated by global market and financial systems. They concluded that they needed to craft a new kind of citizen, one capable of thriving, and enabling the UAE to thrive, in the global economy. In doing so, the Emirates' governing sheikhs faced major challenges. They still had difficulty advancing any compelling ethnocultural account of UAE identity. Their state was historically recent, and though many of their citizens valued older tribal, pan-Arabic, or Muslim identities, too much emphasis on those allegiances could undermine national loyalties. Many proponents of those identities, especially Islamists, criticized the government's economic vision of Emirati peoplehood as a corrupt Western imposition, even as critics attacked these Muslim activists for favoring "foreign" versions of Islam over Emirati traditions.[45] The ruling sheikhs were understandably wary of allying too closely with movements trumpeting those ethnocultural themes.

Moreover, because the UAE does limit access to citizenship and its material benefits, while relying extensively on immigrant labor, UAE citizens are a small, privileged minority within the far larger and more diverse resident alien population of their own country. UAE elites complain that it is hard to give their children a sense of Emirati cultural identity when, for example, so many of those children are raised by Filipina nannies.[46] Nor can the regime easily rely on winning loyalty through political power themes, since its strength lies in wealth, not military forces, and the Emirates' monarchs do not wish to give most of their citizens, much less the country's other residents, any real voice in government.

As a result, the UAE's rulers have had little choice but to try to tweak their economic case for why citizens should value membership in the United Arab Emirates. They have still sought to convince their people that UAE citizenship is a road to wealth, but now it is wealth that the Emirati should earn by becoming "loyal bourgeois" citizens who display "a vigorous entrepreneurial spirit," with lots of "self-reliance and initiative" and a "strong work ethic" (as stated in the government's 2010 strategic plan, *UAE Vision 2021*).[47]

Calvert Jones finds that so far, the UAE's pursuit of this vision has had very mixed success. Younger citizens all too often become, in her phrase, "entitled patriots." They firmly believe that they are exceptional people in an exceptional country that provides its citizens with paths to prosperity and status; but many still prefer to get wealth through government jobs rather than their own business start-ups.[48] Those who do pursue entrepreneurial identities, moreover, particularly those who succeed, often come to see themselves as members of a transnational, cosmopolitan community of global economic elites, rather than primarily as Emirati citizens. The inhabitants of many postcolonial regimes similarly find themselves confronting movements and groups advancing different stories of who they are and where their allegiances should go—to older tribes, to states originally crafted by imperial rulers, to transnational coethnics or fellow religious believers, to global economic enterprises and endeavors, and much more. In such circumstances, it is not surprising that many find it hard to form a clear, sustaining sense of their political peoplehood.

THE PHILIPPINES

The complex challenges that the interactions of colonial legacies, post-imperial state building, and global economic and social networks pose for the maintenance of political identities are also vividly illustrated by Jan Padios's *A Nation on the Line,* which discusses national narratives in the Philippines.[49] Her analysis encompasses Filipina nannies working in places like the UAE; but it focuses on what she calls "the single most important social, cultural, and economic development in the country in the twenty-first century." Aided by state policies, the Philippines have surpassed India to become "the call center capital of the world." By 2015 the Filipino call center industry generated roughly 7.5 percent of the nation's GDP, almost as much as the remittances of all overseas Filipino workers.[50]

Padios's research indicates that this major industry was built in part through promotional narratives stressing that the Philippines' historical status as an American colony has fostered a deep familiarity with American culture, as well as the ability among Filipinos to speak American-style English. These skills enable the country's workers to perform call center services for American customers more effectively than those of any other nation. Industry executives also contend that Filipinos excel in call center work because, just as their American colonial governors used to claim, they have innate cultural traits of compassion and warmth. As one business leader put it, "We are good at working with the heart."[51]

Padios contends that until recently, both government and corporate leaders in the Philippines wove these imperially shaped themes into a proud national claim that Filipinos are uniquely equipped to prosper in the global knowledge economy of the twenty-first century. They also promised that this new Philippines IT service economy would enable overseas Filipina and Filipino workers, like the nannies of the United Arab

Emirates, to return home and care for their own children in their own land. Yet these recent narratives stressing Filipinos' cultural serviceability for Americans inevitably communicate a message of linked identity with, if not continuing dependence on, the United States. Though many Filipinos relish this story, others find it alienating. It can seem to present them as basically adjunct Americans.

It also turns out that there are limits to how far these friendly call centers can take Filipino workers and the nation economically. Those limits may tighten as many call center functions become automated. It is therefore understandable that more recently, an authoritarian nationalist populist, Rodrigo Duterte, has gained power and often deployed anti-American rhetoric, while exploring a closer relationship with China—though he now seems to have found a kindred spirit in President Trump. In different ways, then, the citizens of this postcolonial nation are receiving shifting and contradictory economic, political, and cultural accounts of who they are and what their aspirations should be.

NORTHERN IRELAND

Although the older nation-states of Europe and North America face distinctive difficulties, their current challenges are in some respects less different from those of newer nations than might be expected. All were built in part as internal empires comprising communities that did not wish to be included when these nation-states were new. Many of these communities are dissatisfied with their political statuses today. Peter R. Gardner has shown that in Northern Ireland, long claimed by Great Britain but placed in the northeast corner of what is now the Republic of Ireland, some Protestants have responded to feelings of embattlement and marginalization by championing their ethnic identity as "Ulster-Scots."[52] They have promoted education in their own language, rather than Gaelic or English; and their Ulster-Scots Agency has increasingly insisted that not only are the Ulster-Scots a people many hundreds of years old, they were in fact the prime creators of the United States of America, and most of the best features of American culture.[53]

This new narrative of Ulster-Scots identity as "Ulster-Scots Americanism" does not serve to advance any particular economic strategy, unlike the Philippines' "call center nation" story. Instead, it appears to express a deep "desire for collective dignity" as well as for a "sense of cultural authenticity."[54] Even so, by defining an identity and a loyalty that is in important ways not Irish, not English, and not even clearly British, this Ulster-Scots identity, in Gardner's judgment, "holds considerable capacity for the perpetuation and deepening of senses of communal dissociation" in Ulster.[55] Living amid the deep divisions, anxieties, and animosities created by the historical colonial relationship between Great Britain and Ireland and the attendant conflicts between Catholics and Protestants, those calling themselves Ulster-Scots have chosen to elaborate a story of peoplehood different from all of the above, adding to the great complexities of life in Northern Ireland, even before the difficulties now posed by Brexit.

RURAL WISCONSIN

These experiences of struggling with multiple, conflicting stories of peoplehood are, however, hardly confined to colonial or postcolonial societies, or even the colonized populations within long-established states. In our modern mix of globalization and fragmentation, competing senses of peoplehood have become more visible and politically significant even among—perhaps especially among—long-dominant groups in the oldest modern nations. They are the ones who most fervently embrace populist politics in many nations, including the United States. Kathy Cramer, in *The Politics of Resentment,* uses thoughtful observations of informal conversations to describe the political perspectives of rural Wisconsin citizens, many of whom voted first for the populist, antiestablishment Republican Scott Walker, and then for the still more antiestablishment Donald Trump.[56]

Cramer finds that the "rural consciousness" prevalent in Wisconsin today has three major components that map well onto the typical themes in stories of peoplehood. She contends that many rural Wisconsinites see themselves as part of a distinctive community that does not receive its "fair share of decision-making power," or its "fair share of public resources," and that is also "distinct from urban (and suburban) areas in their culture and lifestyle."[57] These represent, respectively, a political power theme, an economic theme, and a constitutive identity theme. These rural people believe they do more genuine hard work, with their hands and backs, and that they are more moral, neighborly people than those they see as urban elites who neither know nor care about their problems. Rural Wisconsin folks pride themselves on being givers, not takers. Yet they are resentful because they feel they receive far fewer material rewards than city people do, and that they are disdained as "hicks" and "rednecks."[58] Though their story of rural political peoplehood blends all three themes, recently they have most pressed their political power concerns, their beliefs that the governing officials, bureaucrats, and university experts in the capitol in Madison give them no effective voice in the decisions shaping their lives. Partly as a result, they voted for Walker and Trump, who told them they were right to feel aggrieved and promised to be their champions against the elite objects of their resentment.

To be sure, rural grievances against urbanites are not new, in the United States or elsewhere. It is also certain that most rural Wisconsinites today still see themselves not just as "rural people" but as "Wisconsin citizens" and "U.S. citizens," among many other identities. Still, both their conversations, as reported by Cramer, and their recent voting behavior suggest that rural Wisconsinites' sense of themselves as having a distinct and unjustly treated political identity is far stronger than in much of the past. Their "rural political peoplehood" is shaping, and challenging, their "Wisconsin" and "American" peoplehood more than at many other times.

There are good reasons for this. As Cramer notes, though many rural Wisconsin people choose to scapegoat groups for their problems who are not plausibly responsible for them, they do have real problems. In Wisconsin and in many other places, rural populations are a smaller share of the population, and more demographically distinct from the growing numbers of city dwellers, than they have ever been. At the same time, modern communications mean they are less isolated from those cities and the broader world than they have ever been, so that all the economic and cultural differences are in view. When they contend that people in power are, for example, tailoring educational curriculum and student transportation policies for the needs of suburban and urban populations rather than addressing the distinctive problems of rural regions, they are generally not mistaken. It is therefore not surprising that rural Wisconsinites are telling stories, and showing they can be mobilized by stories, portraying them as a distinct, virtuous, wrongly neglected people. It is also unsurprising that they cheer for mechanistic populist narratives of Wisconsin and American citizenship in which they are once again central actors and central beneficiaries—stories that promise they can be great again.

The rural/urban divide is just one of many axes around which distinct and conflicting senses of political peoplehood are now forming. Even if all politics has always been identity politics, today we live in an era of extraordinarily multifaceted identity politics, as an avalanche of journalism and scholarship has shown. Again, if we are to grasp this era fully, we cannot focus on nation-states alone. Today important players in the politics of peoplehood include social movements championing racial identities, like Black Lives Matter and the American Indian Movement; communities of shared interest and identity defined by disabilities, sexuality, and other traits sometimes defined as cultural, such as the deaf community and the LGBTQ community; and a huge variety of traditional ethnic and immigrant groups. We must also recognize that the transnational NGOs and advocacy groups that Haass and others stress are also identity politics practitioners. They speak for workers, environmentalists, diaspora communities, cosmopolitans favoring human rights and international justice institutions, and religious communities, within and across national borders, among many more. Identity politics themes are also highly prominent in the separatist regional movements that are today far more widespread than is often recognized. At this writing they include, for example, insurgent efforts in Cameroon, Corsica, Flanders, Kurdistan, Nagorna-Karabakh in Azerbaijan, and Transnistra in Moldova, along with perhaps more globally visible movements in Scotland, Quebec, Catalonia, and Tibet. This list could be greatly extended.

Furthermore, though centuries-old examples like the Hudson's Bay Company and the East India Company show that roles for corporations in shaping global political developments are far from new, Shaun Breslin and others are right to call for heightened attention to the political roles modern multinational corporations are playing.[59] Some have annual revenues that exceed those of most states, and many strive to foster strong senses of allegiance in their employees, chiefly but by no means exclusively through economic stories. The identities they nurture can mean that "their people" behave more as corporate loyalists than as national citizens. Google's website, for example, states: "Our mission is to organize the world's information and make it universally accessible and useful," because the company is "dedicated to creating opportunity for everyone"—so the website heralds Google's work in many lands, in cosmopolitan fashion.[60]

Moreover, not only do most of today's social movements, advocacy groups, cultural associations, religious communities, regional autonomy or separatism proponents, and multinational corporations suggest at times that their members should give their loyalties first and foremost to them, and only secondarily to the frequently ineffective governments of the states they inhabit. They also transmit those suggestions far more rapidly, more widely, more frequently, and through more media than ever before. In so doing, they contribute mightily to the noisy roar of identity stories that has become the soundtrack of modern everyday life.

And they will not soon be shouted down. There is no real likelihood that any overarching global story of friends and enemies will emerge in the near future to provide the kind of order, structure, and stability to our multiple political identities that the Cold War once did. The ubiquitous concerns about terrorism throughout the world do not fill this gap. When much of the world openly embraced communism, while much of the rest of the world celebrated capitalism, there was a clear structure of opposed identities and alliances on both sides. But today, virtually all states and peoples profess to oppose terrorism. They simply disagree vigorously about which groups really are terrorists, and which are valiant freedom fighters or noble servants of a holy cause. Even states' own designations of groups as terrorists or as heroes can shift rapidly. Witness Ronald Reagan's fervent praise and aid in the 1980s for the Afghani mujahedeen, some of whom later became the less beloved Taliban; and the CIA's early employment of Saddam Hussein, later compared by former CIA director George H. W. Bush to Hitler.

All this means that few people can bring order to the modern world's conflicting claims of political identities simply by deciding whether they are for or against terrorism, as they once could by deciding whether they were for communism or the self-proclaimed "free world." People instead are engulfed by information about innumerable different political communities and associations. Many feel pulled and pushed in different directions. It is reasonable to conclude that this cacophony of political stories, accompanying the extensive economic and cultural transformations of recent years, has added to the appeal of the stridently nationalist forms of populism that are now so prominent.

For despite all that has changed, it remains true that the most dominant, familiar stories of political peoplehood for most of the world's inhabitants are narratives of nation-states. These stories still resonate deeply with billions of people, even if their states appear ineffective, embattled, and corrupt. They are stories that can readily be told with a simplicity, clarity, and authority that proponents of rival senses of political identity often can manage only with great difficulty. It is also easy to tell stories of the plight of many modern nation-states in ways that assign blame for their problems on the forces of economic globalization, on racial, ethnic, and religious minorities and immigrants, on everything and everyone that appears to be making the nation less than its members imagine it once was, and less than they would like it to be. Their great capacity to tell compelling political stories is one reason why nationalist populists around the world now believe that tomorrow belongs to them.

We therefore must consider not only the ways that economic and cultural changes are constructing the landscape of contemporary politics, but also the ways that clashing stories of peoplehood are multiplying, and at the same time dividing us, in order to grasp the challenges we face. We can then see more clearly why pathological forms of populism—narrowly nationalistic, racial, and religious, exclusionary and repressive stories of who the people are and why they deserve to rule—are having such broad and deep resonance in many parts of the world today. But based on that recognition, we can also begin to form some ideas of how we can best respond to the concerns and aspirations that drive these pathological populisms.

2

What Makes a Good Story of Peoplehood?

Today pundits, politicians, and citizens in many lands are advancing ideas about how to respond to the dangers of pathological forms of populism. Social scientists tend to focus on exploring causal explanations rather than suggesting solutions, but the urgency of current concerns has prompted some also to offer political prescriptions. Just as I broadly agree with most of the prevalent diagnoses of the economic and cultural sources of contemporary pathological populisms, I broadly agree with many recent recommendations.

Even valuable suggestions, however, are too often wrapped in very indefinite conceptions of desirable political communities that compete poorly with more concrete and vivid, if often narrowly nationalistic, populisms. Most academic responses focus on moral principles and on policies said to be right from a putatively universal point of view, largely detached from the perspective of any particular country. Many scholars especially shy away from articulating desirable national stories for the societies that are increasingly under the sway of populist appeals. They do so for understandable, even commendable reasons. Nonetheless, their works leave us groping for ways to carry out the necessary intellectual and political project of opposing bad stories of political peoplehood with better ones. In this chapter I lay out several criteria for doing so.

Prevailing Responses

Though each writer is distinctive in certain ways, many of the current responses to pathological forms of populism stress three arguments:

First, most contend that desirable national identities must be fundamentally "civic" or liberal democratic. This means those identities must rest on an ideology that champions commitments to democracy and human rights that are portrayed as universal principles, rather than "blood and soil" conceptions of a nation or a people.

Second, most nonetheless argue that these liberal democratic national identities must reflect the distinctive cultural traditions prevalent in particular societies. This second response poses a problem for the first. How distinctive can desirable national identities be if they all rest on commitments to the same principles of liberal democracy? Most writers display some awareness of this fundamental tension in their arguments, but few address it fully.

Third, many analysts instead focus on reviewing the economic and cultural grievances that they see as driving populist movements; and then they offer a list of economic and social policies to ameliorate those grievances. The economic policies generally seek to promote greater employment, wages, and benefits, while the social policies focus on finding compromises with the opponents of demographic diversity and increased immigration levels. These authors are right to think that good policies must be part of all effective responses to pathological populisms. But policies are less persuasive—they can seem like arbitrary laundry lists—when they do not gain meaning and legitimacy from a broader narrative of national identity and purpose.

Consider a few recent examples. In *The People vs. Democracy: Why Our Freedom Is in Danger and How to Save It,* Yascha Mounk calls for "defenders of liberal democracy" to offer "a positive message" to "rival the narrative according to which" only illiberal populists can fix a nation's problems. This positive message should be articulated in a "new language of inclusive patriotism" that builds "on the tradition of multiethnic democracy to show that the ties that bind us go well beyond ethnicity and religion." The desirable ties are the "basic tenets of liberal democracy," which should be rhetorically celebrated, inculcated through culturally appropriate civic education programs, and strengthened by public and private policies to realize them more fully. Toward that end, Mounk calls for changes in tax and housing policies; investments in education; and a restructuring of welfare states and work to provide both greater economic security and more meaningful employment opportunities. He reluctantly calls for some policy compromises with anti-immigration forces, but he cautions against jettisoning "the universal promises of liberal democracy in favor of rights and duties rooted in particular ethnic or religious communities."[1]

Mounk's well-crafted arguments conform fairly completely to the three elements I sketched above. Regarding the core difficulty of this formula, however—the tension between favoring a universalistic ideological conception of civic identity and supporting the development of a distinctive national culture—Mounk's response is mainly to admonish that the second must not be allowed to erode the first. Though his subtitle speaks of "Our Freedom," it is never entirely clear who that "Our" includes—all Americans? All liberal democrats? All humanity? Consequently, many may feel uncertain whether Mounk is really speaking to or for them.

In *Anti-Pluralism: The Populist Threat to Liberal Democracy,* William Galston adheres to the same basic formula, differing chiefly in some of his policy recommendations. He makes it clear from the outset, however, that his concern is with all countries that base their identities on civic commitments to "liberal democracy." These, he cautions, now face "deformations" from both "elitists" and antipluralist "populist movements." He calls on leaders in every liberal democratic nation to combat those deformations by articulating "the public culture of their community," its "distinctive . . . set of beliefs that amalgamate principle, shared history, and distinctive ethnicities," with the goal of helping "the people to unite around the fundamentals of their civic identity." Galston's examples include the "deep patriotism" of speeches by Martin Luther King Jr., Franklin Roosevelt, and Ronald Reagan.

Galston also advocates for economic policies designed to produce full employment with rising wages, and to connect residents of small towns and rural regions with the opportunities now found in cities. Like Mounk, he calls for compromises with anti-immigration forces, in his case by "shifting away from family reunification and toward economic contribution as the main criterion for immigration," along with a greater focus on helping immigrants learn English and gain "a working knowledge of American history and civic institutions." But this is as far as Galston goes in clarifying how he would deal with the tension between the first and second prongs of the standard response to pathological populisms. He does not seek to explain how leaders can or should "amalgamate" the general principles of liberal democracy with the "distinctive ethnicities" and other particular features of individual nations.[2]

Finally, in *Identity: The Demand for Dignity and the Politics of Resentment,* Francis Fukuyama presents another variant of the same response. He too contends that we need "creedal national identities built around the foundational ideas of modern liberal democracy." He adds, however, "a creedal identity is a necessary but not a sufficient condition for success." It requires support from "its own culture, which must be held in higher esteem than cultures rejecting democracy's values." Acknowledging the importance of "stories of peoplehood" in this regard, Fukuyama suggests that "a progressive narrative" can be told, in America at least, "about the overcoming of barriers and ever-broadening circles of people whose dignity the country has recognized, based on its founding principles." But he says nothing more about what crafting and advancing such narratives entails. Instead, he repeatedly stresses that the core task is to define "a proper creedal identity." And he, too, devotes most of his attention to arguing for economic policies that can "mitigate concerns over jobs, incomes, and security," even as he urges compromises with opponents of immigration. He particularly stresses sanctions against employers of undocumented aliens, calling for "public policies to deliberately assimilate newcomers" to liberal cultural values through not just civic education but also more demanding naturalization tests, and perhaps a "universal requirement for national service."[3]

I agree with all these authors that we need to strengthen commitments to democracy and human rights, and to adopt economic and social policies that will more fully realize those commitments in people's lives, responding to current popular grievances. Though I disagree with some of their policy proposals, as they do among themselves, I seek not to oppose their broadly kindred endeavors, only to add to them by focusing on what makes a good story of peoplehood. I believe this focus will help writers to clarify the "we" to whom and for whom they are writing; explain how best to articulate liberal democratic commitments within particular traditions of national identity;

and delineate how a national culture can be valued without fostering xenophobia. By so doing, advocates can lessen, though not eliminate, the tension between civic identities based on abstract principles and the promotion of distinctive, inevitably more particular political identities and cultures.

Are Better Stories Possible?

Admittedly, there are reasons to doubt that the route I am recommending is open to us. David Ricci has recently argued in two books that modern liberalism, along with positions farther to the left, displays crippling constitutive features that partly explain liberal democrats' difficulties in responding to exclusionary, repressive populisms. He contends that, unlike conservatives, liberals are often unwilling to tell, and may be unable to tell, narratives of national identity that respond symbolically to popular desires for feelings of secure belonging, pride, and solidarity, and that guide practical policies to help meet those desires.[4] Precisely because modern liberal democrats profess to value cultural, racial, ethnic, and religious diversity, while they rest political legitimacy on conformity to principles of democracy and human rights that they deem universal, many are uncomfortable with celebrations of the history and characteristics of a nation's traditionally dominant groups, and with measures designed to address those groups' concerns. They see all particularistic stories of national peoplehood as first steps down a slippery slope to intolerant chauvinism.

Most liberals, according to Ricci, also esteem forms of scientific rationality that challenge the myths and providentialist histories that national narratives often espouse. In their eyes, to endorse most national stories of peoplehood is to believe in preposterous, self-interested fables. Many liberals today have come to see the whole world system of sovereign, independent nation-states as an archaic structure of political and economic power and institutions that inherently breeds bigotry and indefensible inequalities. Today's world of sovereign nation-states, they believe, must give way eventually to more cosmopolitan and confederated forms of democracy, if not a global federal republic.

I share many of these concerns. My own political commitments were inspired by the civil rights and women's movements of the 1960s and 1970s, on the one hand, and by disillusionment with the militarism and intolerance of the Cold War and its consequences in Vietnam, on the other. Still, embarrassing as it is to confess, the sight that most fired my youthful political imagination came in 1966, when I first laid eyes on the bridge of the Starship *Enterprise,* as it appeared in the first season of *Star Trek.* The crew were officers of an amazing interstellar federal republic, the United Federation of Planets. They included individuals from America's World War II enemy, Japan (Lieutenant Sulu); its Cold War rival, Russia (Ensign Chekov); an African American woman (Lieutenant Uhura); and even a true alien (First Officer Spock), a Vulcan who looked sinister but who presumably was documented. Setting reassuring boundaries to all this radicalism, the captain was a swaggering white Iowan, James T. Kirk. He and the ship's chief engineer, Montgomery Scott, and its chief medical officer, Leonard McCoy, were all of at least partly Scottish descent (as was I). Corny as all this sounds now, in 1966 the sight of these diverse people working together as equals on a mission of scientific exploration launched by the most cosmopolitan federal republic imaginable seemed a pathbreaking vision of the pursuit of the finest Enlightenment ideals. In truth, I would still love to take that journey.

As the recent surge of exclusionary, repressive nationalistic movements shows, however, we are a long way away from doing so. Moreover, liberal discourses that naively presume this vision to be obviously the normatively right one for humanity, as I once did, can be active impediments to moving in this direction. Ricci is right that the rhetoric of these discourses often fails to appeal to people and groups who feel harmed by economic globalization and cosmopolitan multiculturalism, and who hold more traditionalist views, including many conventional forms of religion and patriotism. Liberal rhetorics often convey disdain for such groups and their beliefs and values, fostering understandable resentments.

Yet though disagreements are inevitable, there is no reason to conclude that the causes of democracy, human rights, and the improvement of human well-being in other regards must be articulated in counterproductive ways. There is no reason liberals cannot tell compelling political stories, even though it is true that they now often fail to do so. Liberal democratic values have, to be sure, not proven to be hegemonic enough to bring about the end of humanity's history of ideological conflicts. Still, in today's world, virtually every community has at least some members with both awareness and respect for those values, who can be expected to respond favorably to narratives embodying them. Yet in each community the historic contexts of obstacles to democracy and human rights differ; the institutional forms favored to advance democracy and human rights differ; and the struggles over whether to do so differ. This mix of shared values and contextual differences means that every political society has within it materials to craft a distinctive story, or multiple overlapping stories, of how its values and identity reflect specific understandings of liberal democratic commitments, and distinctive challenges and opportunities for their realization, alongside its members' other goals.

It is wise, moreover, for those liberals who believe that their principles ultimately point toward the transcendence of allegiances to existing nation-states to use narratives of their political communities and identities to show how such transcendence can fulfill the best values present in existing nation-states, rather than simply urging their disavowal. Beginning with national stories does not necessarily imply ending with them.[5] It instead means, as I argue below, starting with values, identities, and concerns that people can recognize as their own.

It is true that stories that suggest we should move beyond the geographic and social boundaries of existing communities are likely to be heard as threatening by many who feel strongly attached to existing arrangements. This perception of threat may well foster conflicts. That danger cannot be wholly avoided; but there are ways to offer compelling accounts of national identities that can lessen it. If liberal democrats believe that people have rights to the pursuit of happiness, for example, and many persons prefer to pursue happiness through the shared lives of subcommunities with distinctive identities and traditions, then it is not just appropriate but mandatory to give considerable deference to their choices. We should seek to understand why they believe those choices are right for them, given their existing senses of who they are and what they should be. We should also consider soberly the costs to the opportunities and respect that others receive if traditionalists act on their beliefs in certain ways, such as maintaining monuments and ceremonial displays in public spaces, using public facilities for group events, refusing some commercial services to those with different values, and claiming exemptions from certain taxes and public duties. As part of efforts to reach broadly acceptable resolutions of the controversies these actions may spur, liberals should explore with different communities whether and in what ways the values they endorse include concerns for democracy and human rights, among other moral commitments. Most often, these explorations will generate awareness of some real common ground, even though differences will persist. Liberal democrats can then work with a wide range of communities to advance desirable values that have a place in each of their distinctive yet not altogether dissimilar stories of peoplehood.

Stories can provide this aid because it is natural for them to incorporate not only current political grievances and challenges and deep senses of identity and affiliation, but also norms born of historic interactions with other groups, in their accounts of both the past and future. Most important, stories can help because they can make membership in a particular political community not only appear to be, but *actually* be, a distinctive, ongoing collective endeavor, and an endeavor that participants can hope to make more broadly and deeply beneficial over time. As scholars like Benedict Anderson, Yuval Harari, and others have shown, when people imagine each other as fellow members of a collective enterprise, their ensuing conduct makes what begins as an imagined enterprise into something material. But this kind of political metamorphosis requires stories that narrate members' shared identity in ways that are concrete enough to be readily grasped, and in which members can clearly see themselves.

So instead of depicting political membership as so many current analysts do, as fundamentally a matter of pledging allegiance to an abstract civic creed, often one that mandates duties that many gloomily feel they cannot fulfill, it is wiser to pursue a different course. Allegiance should go less to a creed than to a shared endeavor that participants can see as expressive of their identities and interests as well as their ideals. Stories of peoplehood inspire us most when they encourage us to think of ourselves as doing what is needed in practice to carry on our particular collective political projects today, even as they allow us to hope that we may do still better tomorrow. Narratives of political identity therefore can enable us to say to proponents of cruelty, "that is not who we are!"—or, at least, "that is not who we want to be or who we are trying to be." If, that is, they are good stories of peoplehood.

How to Compose Good Stories of Peoplehood

What makes political stories good, or at least better than most others? By "good" stories of peoplehood, I mean two things: stories that do a good job of engaging and motivating people, and stories that convey substantive messages that can honestly be judged to be normatively defensible, even commendable, by those who tell and hear them. Only if a story is good in both these ways can it provide a promising means to ease the tension between trying to foster commitments to overarching, if perhaps not truly universal, principles of democracy and rights, while also making a compelling case for the significance of membership in particular political communities. From these two dimensions of what makes political stories good, we can derive criteria for constructing desirable narratives.

THE THREE RS OF STORIES OF PEOPLEHOOD

When I was young, the fundamentals of education were often referred to as the "three Rs": reading, 'riting, and 'rithmetic. We obviously had to strain to call all these elements "Rs," especially the third. Somewhat similarly, three interrelated criteria should guide efforts to develop political stories in and for different communities today. We can call them the "three Rs" of good peoplehood narratives: stories must be *resonant, respectful,* and *reticulated.* Here, too, I am obviously straining to get that third R! Still, the unconventional term "reticulated" is appropriate, because this criterion is the least familiar and most poorly understood of the three. I will argue that reticulation may nonetheless be most important if stories of peoplehood are to be normatively defensible at this time in human history.

It is, however, the first criterion—requiring stories to be resonant—that is most important for ensuring that the concern for normatively desirable stories does not reduce to an insistence that all stories are simply variants of the same creed, grounded on commitments to abstract principles of democracy and human rights. To tell resonant stories, political actors must speak to and from the conceptions of identities and interests already possessed by their audiences. They must do so even when political storytellers seek—as they almost inevitably do—to persuade people to reconceive those identities and interests in some respects. The stories must find a clear and compelling place for people's economic and cultural anxieties and difficulties. They must also articulate community goals and promising policies in which people can see at least some of their most cherished values advanced. As Saul Alinsky–style organizers have long preached, to be effective, would-be political and intellectual leaders must begin by taking people where they are.

Doing so requires a rich knowledge of particular political contexts—the traditions, values, identities, and practices that the inhabitants of a particular area possess and pursue, as well as the challenges they face. The resulting stories of peoplehood will inevitably be significantly different for different populations in different places and at different times, since those populations will always vary in their preexisting identities, histories, and current challenges. Those stories therefore can place more abstract commitments to democracy and justice within a narrative that people can recognize as uniquely their own, and they should do so to win support. Gaining support is not, however, the only reason. They should do so because it is right to convey truthfully to constituents the ways in which who they now are and what they now value are central parts of the imagined community they are being asked to embrace. And generally, the moral perspectives of political actors who offer stories to their communities themselves originated with the traditions and histories upon which they are building. It is intellectually honest to tell stories that acknowledge and express this reality.

In this regard, my argument is in the vein of Michael Walzer's conception of normative prescription as, at its most truthful, connected social criticism—the fruits of efforts to interpret the experiences, identities, and moral values we initially find in our social worlds, and then reason on the basis of the most persuasive understandings of them we can reach.[6] Those understandings may or may not eventually take the form of appeal to what we regard as universal principles of reason, or perhaps divine revelation. Universal principles or revelations are not the starting point, however, for treating the values in particular social realms as concerns we should take seriously. The starting points are the beliefs of the people whose identities a story of peoplehood seeks both to articulate and shape. Yet even if we begin with the moral traditions and understandings prevalent in actual communities today, this connected, critical engagement with people's experiences and values will often prompt us to elaborate stories in which concerns for democracy, human dignity, and basic human rights have prominent places. Again, those values are now present, though not dominant, almost everywhere. Resonant stories will therefore generally have to take account of them along with, indeed as part of, a people's particular history and traditions. By beginning both with constituents' unique identities, values, concerns, and aspirations, and with the types of liberal democratic norms that have won recognition in their locales, stories of peoplehood will have greater political efficacy, and they will blend more local and more cosmopolitan values more convincingly. And in so doing, they will better conform to the normative requirement imposed by the second R: they will be respectful.

What does this second criterion entail? Whom must stories of peoplehood respect? How and why? The answers to these questions always have been highly contested. Still, in the twenty-first century, these contests take place on material and moral planes with different horizons from those that once prevailed in many parts of the world. It makes a great difference that most people now have better and more rapid access to news and stories about people elsewhere than they did through most of human history. Today, few can escape awareness of at least some of the challenges facing people in remote regions. They also cannot avoid being conscious of religious, philosophical, moral, legal, and political traditions that assign inestimable value to the dignity of every human being. Most identify with at least some of those traditions. Frequently their governments are signatories to international treaties that commit them to respect for human rights and democratic self-governance.[7] Journalists, advocacy groups, religious leaders, and sometimes other states can and do bring pressure to live up to those commitments. So it is almost always possible to maintain to people that many of their own values strongly support respect for all human beings. It is often, though not always, even easier to insist that their states should respect all of the people over whom they assert the rightful power to govern, even if not all humanity.

In almost every context, moreover, most people agree that respect requires, first, giving some minimal hearing to people's voices, to their concerns, hopes, and fears. It is impossible to claim to respect people to whom one refuses to listen. Respect means, second, engaging with people in a spirit of accommodation whenever possible. It means accepting that others are entitled to pursue their preferred ways of life, unless we feel we must judge their ways illegitimate or harmful.

That "unless" is, to be sure, a major limitation on respect. In some communities, practices that other communities permit or even esteem, such as cross-ethnic marriages, are deemed repugnant, and the communities that allow them are seen as too foreign or decadent to merit respect. Virtually every community also displays intense internal disagreements over the legitimacy of some members' preferred pursuits, making respect for all within the community hard to sustain. Yet we can find almost everywhere values and traditions arguing that even if certain pursuits are ultimately to be condemned, still all persons, and certainly those whom governments seek to govern, initially deserve basic respect. Consequently, those narrating stories of peoplehood can virtually always tell stories that insist on respect for the dignity, values, and concerns of all whom they are likely to affect, in ways that resonate with their audiences' own moral commitments.

Precisely because the second criterion calls for narratives that express respect for the diverse ways of life pursued by the individuals and communities they describe, it leads in turn to the third criterion. To be deemed good stories of peoplehood, narratives must be reticulated. They must openly embrace, in two distinct and equally important regards, a significant measure of pluralism within the shared life of the society whose stories they tell.

"Reticulated" is a term for networks that display discernible, though not always predictable, patterns among the elements that constitute a larger whole. These patterns transform jumbles of differences into more orderly and attractive arrangements that generally have more utility and durability. Reticulation thus stands in contrast both to undifferentiated uniformity and to chaotic disorder. Good stories of peoplehood should help weave networks with two kinds of legible patterns, one internal to the stories, one external. Internally, in accordance with the criterion of respect, narratives should not demand civic homogeneity, which can only be achieved, as James Madison knew, by extinguishing liberty.[8] Instead they should not just accept but actively facilitate pluralism. They should authorize accommodations of a people's subgroups, such as minority religions, geographic regions, indigenous communities, persons with unconventional sexualities, the disabled, and more, to the greatest degree possible, consistent with the constitutive themes central to that particular account of peoplehood. These accommodations can take many forms, including federalism, special representation in legislatures, exemptions from generally binding laws, and making public services more widely accessible, among other measures. Those accommodations of differences should, however, be limited by concerns to preserve places and structures that can appropriately sustain others within the reticulated whole that comprises a society.

Similarly, externally, stories should convey openness to compromising with, and often allying with, the communities, policies, and institutions advanced by advocates of distinct but overlapping stories of peoplehood, whenever they have areas of agreement. They should accept that their society's institutions and policies are therefore more likely to be a network of shifting patterns emerging from evolving areas of agreement among many stories, rather than rigid, unchanging arrangements. This spirit of external accommodation should extend to receptivity to membership in regional and international institutions and alliances when these are well suited to advance a people's economic welfare, political power, and constitutive values.

Precisely because the call to embrace reticulated visions of political communities inescapably is a call to accept significant diversity, it is a call that many, particularly those drawn to highly nationalistic forms of populism, will fiercely resist. Even though some commitments to democracy and human rights are now present in most places around the world, they are far from hegemonic in many of them. Indeed, they are not wholly accepted anywhere. Thus it may seem that if we try to compose stories of peoplehood that resonate with dominant local traditions and identities, often we just won't end up with narratives that display respect for all, or willingness to accommodate diverse groups within a society or alliances with others.

Perhaps. Yet if we presume that to be the case, without exploring the possibilities for better narratives, we verge on concluding that there can be no response to narrowly nationalist populisms except all-out efforts to destroy them. I believe those efforts are at least as likely to fail as an approach that seeks to find as much common ground as possible with all groups, including populist traditionalists. Arguably, modern liberals have lost more support and gained more enemies by being dismissive toward those who do not share all their beliefs than by being too open to accommodations. Too often, it is liberals who fear real diversity the most.

We also should not set the bar too high for when we can find advancing resonant, respectful, and reticulated stories of peoplehood to be worthwhile. I make no claim that we can always and everywhere find ways of composing stories that are sure to defeat all champions of antipluralist, authoritarian forms of populism. Nothing is certain in politics. But I believe we can see in every context the potential for stories of this sort to be serious political competitors. Because of the diversity that already exists in many societies, in most there are already some minorities who are publicly embraced, even if others are disdained. These examples set precedents for the feasibility of still broader inclusiveness. And because political leaders, parties, and movements in most societies pay at least lip service to feeling concern for all whom they wish to govern, they almost always invoke some more inclusive as well as more exclusionary moral traditions. They then can feel pressures to live up to them.

In the remainder of this chapter, I seek to make this claim plausible by noting the potential for better stories of peoplehood in a few of the countries around the world where pathological forms of populism are powerful today. Three things will be clear in every case. First, nationalist populists are advancing clear, strong stories of their country's distinctive identity that appear to contribute greatly to their success. Second, those stories have predictable mechanistic structures and constitutive themes. Over and over again leaders tell those whose loyalty they wish to inspire that their nation was once highly accomplished, happy, and moral, if it was not indeed the greatest in the world. Then corrupt selfish elites plunged it into danger by departing from the nation's cultural identity and greatness. Only if the "true" people of the nation, or their representatives, are in power will the country ever be great and happy again. This message is generally presented as an iron law of history.

Yet third, in every case, even the narratives of identity advanced by right-leaning populists reveal that today, few if any national stories can be told without paying respect to values of democracy, diversity, and human rights. Each country's history and current circumstances therefore really do provide materials for advancing different, more inclusive, more egalitarian, and more widely respectful national stories. I am, to be sure, not a deeply connected social critic of any of these countries, so I can discuss them only tentatively, in the hopes that others with more knowledge about these societies will be able to work out how to do better. In the next chapter, I will offer a more developed argument about how we can and must tell better stories of peoplehood in America, my own and native land.

BETTER STORIES OF OTHER PEOPLES

Let us first consider Denmark, a nation that regularly scores at or near the top of the rankings of the happiest countries on earth.[9] Happy as they may be overall, the Danes have over the past decade and a half given increasing support to an anti-immigration, self-proclaimed populist party, the Danish People's Party. Since 2015, it has been the second-largest party in the Danish parliament. Its calls for restrictive immigration and naturalization policies, as well as civic education systems that will actively foster Danish culture, have shifted the positions of other Danish parties toward the DPP's preferences.[10] The party's leaders depict these positions as the latest episode in a long and stirring story of the Danes' struggles to maintain their identity. As one put it: "Denmark has a more than thousand year history, based on the Danish people's ongoing battle to exist in spite of unfavorable geographic and strategic circumstances."[11]

The Danish People's Party is a more successful offshoot of the older, economically focused, antitax and anti–government spending Progress Party. The Progress Party was not so fervently nationalistic. In contrast, from its start the DPP has stood on a platform whose essence, according to party leader Kristian Thulesen Dahl, "is a warm and strong love of our country."[12] Its manifesto contains economic and political power themes, but it focuses on constitutive values of "our Danish cultural heritage," which "must be preserved and strengthened." The party defines that culture as "the sum of the Danish people's history, experience, beliefs, language and customs." Among those customs, the Danish People's Party stresses "Denmark's constitutional monarchy" as part of the nation's system of representative government, and the Danish Evangelical Lutheran Church, which the party wants "the government to support" without prejudicing "ordinary religious freedom." The party also places great importance on maintaining Denmark's sovereignty. It opposes the European Union, though not NATO, as a threat to that sovereignty, and it is steadfastly against large-scale immigration, insisting that it "will not accept transformation to a multiethnic society."[13]

The Danish People's Party is not, however, opposed to Denmark's extensive social welfare state, funded through income taxes that have averaged more than 60 percent during the past quarter century.[14] The party accepts health care as a public responsibility, and it endorses a public education system, provided there is "free choice between state and private schools." Unlike many conservative populist parties, it calls for taking "care of the natural world" so that future generations can "live in a clean and healthy environment." It promises to "play an active role in representative government," working "more than happily in cooperation with other parties," so that the "country and its democracy may evolve freely." It also pledges its support for "the fundamental liberties of speech, the right of assembly and religious liberty," as well as the "Danish State Community," the vestige of Denmark's former empire that accords a significant measure of autonomous home rule to Greenland and the Faroe Islands.[15]

The Danish People's Party, in sum, explicitly advances a story of Danish peoplehood structured to present the cultural identity and traditions that were the source of the nation's past happiness and greatness as under threat, now especially from immigration and multiculturalism as well as the bureaucrats of the European Union. Yet it also embraces economic themes that would sound social democratic in the United States. Its political power themes stress both active participation in local and national representative democratic institutions, cooperation with parties with other views whenever possible, and even a reticulated recognition of special status for the "Greenland and Faeroese peoples."[16] It also endorses a range of individual rights. Rather than seeking to become an authoritarian populist dictator, its longtime leader, Kristian Thulesen Dahl, has chosen not to pursue becoming prime minister.

The party's right-wing character is in fact found almost exclusively in its cultural themes, which are, to be sure, its signature ones: its calls for restrictions on immigration and for demanding naturalization policies, with particular opposition to Muslim immigrants; its aversion to multiculturalism and multiethnicity generally; and its emphasis on supporting the national Christian church and monarchy. The appeal of these positions is understandable in light of Danish history and, particularly, the challenges posed by Denmark's membership in the European Union and by the broader forces of economic and cultural globalization.

Alarms about these challenges resonate because they express long-established and widely held views of Danish identity. A leading nineteenth-century version of Danish history, influenced by Romantic thought and identified with an enormously popular book by the historian C. F. Allen, presented the Danes as an ancient, culturally homogeneous and democratic peasant people who for centuries suffered from the emergence of a repressive nobility, foreign religious influences, and periods of foreign rule. Then, beginning in 1849, the creation of a constitutional monarchy with a representative parliament and a national Christian church restored democracy, national sovereignty, and cultural unity.[17] This is essentially the story the Danish People's Party tells today.

Yet this story is far from uncontested among Danes. Modern writers have shown that Denmark was in fact a conglomerate, multinational, multilingual monarchy until its 1864 defeat in a war with Prussia, which led to its loss of Slesvig, Holstein, and Lauenberg and a new period of nation-state building.[18] Subsequently, a peasant movement successfully sought to strengthen Danish agriculture through the creation of cooperatives, to which virtually all Danish farmers still belong. This agricultural movement allied in the late nineteenth century with an educational movement led by Nikolaj F. S. Grundtvig, who fostered the creation of People's High Schools to inculcate an egalitarian sense of Danish peoplehood. Workers' movements also gave rise to the Danish Social Democrats, who came to present socialism as an expression of the solidarity that should characterize the Danish nation-state. The Danish peasant and worker movements, often at odds, eventually came together after World War II in support of the high-tax, high–social provision Danish welfare state. At that point, the cultural scholar Ove Korsgaard argues, "Welfare and Danishness became one and the same. To be Danish was (and still is) to identify oneself with the Danish welfare project."[19]

These accounts structure the story of Danish identity in more teleological terms, as the coming together over time of disparate parts into the shared enterprise of providing welfare and happiness to all, an endeavor that Danes can profitably continue to pursue into the indefinite future. Korsgaard and others contend, however, that subsequent developments have laid siege to this sense of Danish peoplehood. The Danes' decisions to join the European Economic Community and then the European Union, while retaining their own currency, have raised questions about whether Danish peoplehood can survive deeper immersion in a European identity. EU policies have also facilitated immigration into Denmark, including some Muslims. Immigrants of all sorts now make up just under 9 percent of the Danish population and workforce.[20] Though this amount is not huge, it is sufficient to shake the strong sense of cultural solidarity and economic partnership that has underpinned Danish willingness to accept high taxes in return for extensive social welfare benefits. Newcomers who have not long paid into the tax system, and who may not share the native Danes' feelings of solidarity that create trust that all will do their share, seem to be demanding equal treatment with the longtime partners in that Danish welfare project. Beyond these concerns, some Danes feel that as a small nation within the EU and other regional and global institutions, in which participation requires that they learn English, because the world will never learn Danish, their distinctive cultural identity is in danger of being eclipsed within one or two generations. These feelings explain why the DPP's constitutive themes are so potent.

The cultural anxieties and the fears of economic burdens and political insignificance that the DPP's story addresses all richly merit attention. Still, the party's manifesto itself shows that values of democracy, human rights, even a measure of autonomous self-governance for at least some distinct communities, also all have great resonance in Denmark. Even if it is a myth that ancient Danes were a democratic peasant nation, it is not a myth that many Danes have long valued stories of themselves as a deeply democratic people. Furthermore, some writers maintain, Denmark's older history of being a multiethnic, multilingual society deserves recognition as a proud heritage and a source of guidance as Danes seek to cope with greater immigration today.[21] This heritage suggests that Danes have historically found ways to embrace diversity and still flourish. And if, as sociologist Richard Jenkins suggests, modern Danes particularly value the national flag, the Dannebrog; their constitutional monarchy; and the Danish language as symbols of their peoplehood, it should be possible for liberal Danes to advance an egalitarian and inclusive story of peoplehood, probably one devoted to carrying forward the nation's historic and highly successful social welfare project, in which all these treasured elements have a place.[22]

If that seems too sanguine, note that the core cultural value that Grundtvigians taught in the People's High Schools, according to historian Claus Møller Jørgensen, was *folkelighed,* defined as "tolerance, openness, liberalmindedness; the means to achieve *folkelighed* is enlightenment and committed dialogue aimed at consensus."[23] It does not seem far-fetched to say that as the Danish People's Party pushes immigration concerns to the point of anti-Muslim bigotry, visible in measures to ban the burqa and niqab; mark out "ghetto areas"; and require naturalized citizens to shake the hands of their mayors, other Danes can insist, "That is not who we are."[24] Perhaps they can tell a contrasting story depicting Danish peoplehood as devoted to a distinctive yet exemplary democratic social welfare project characterized by folkelighed: openness and tolerance.[25] This story should include policies to ensure that all who benefit from that project really contribute to it; but it is likely that most immigrants will take pride in doing so. Though there are no guarantees of success, it is not hopeless to try. After all, despite everything, most Danes are still happy.

India—the world's largest constitutional democracy since its postcolonial founding in 1947—is a still more challenging case. From independence through the 1980s, the Congress Party of Nehru and the Gandhis dominated Indian elections. Congress Party preeminence then waned, and the Bharatiya Janata Party or BJP, a right-leaning Hindu nationalist party, gained increased support. In 2014, under the leadership of Narendra Modi, the BJP at last won a governing majority in India's Parliament, as well as control of many state governments. It has shaped India's course since then.[26]

The election manifesto, written by Manohar Joshi, that helped bring the BJP to power lays out a forceful story of Indian peoplehood, contending that to "build a modern India," the "best foundation is our own Culture."[27] The manifesto's preface says the "BJP recognizes that no nation could chart out its . . . policies unless it has a clear understanding about itself, its history, its roots, its strengths and failings." It identifies many strengths, proclaiming that "India is the most ancient civilization of the world and has always been looked upon by the world as a land of wealth and wisdom." Before "the advent of the Britishers," it asserts, "India had a much bigger role and presence in industry and manufacturing than any nation in Europe and Asia." India was, in those days, "a land of abundance, prosperity, affluence, a land of sharing and caring living in perfect harmony and peace with the nature. From ancient times, almost all religions practiced in different parts of the world, have existed peacefully in India and will continue to do so. India thus provides the most ennobling experience in spiritual co-existence."[28]

Then, the manifesto indicates, the oppressive British came (as in fact the Muslim Mughal emperors had before them, though this goes unnoted). Against the British, Joshi wrote, the leaders of the "Indian freedom struggle" kept "the Indian ways and thoughts in the centre of their action. They had a vision to reconstruct the political and economic institutions of India as a continuum of civilizational consciousness, which made India one country, one people, and one Nation." After independence, however, "the leaders at the helm of affairs . . . lost the spirit and the vision . . . and adopted the institutional framework . . . created by the Britishers which was quite alien to India's world-view." This decline produced "a multi-dimensional crisis." It included "rising disparities, social and communal divide and terrorism leading to a fractured society." But at its heart were "concentration of power in a few hands" and "lack of people's participation," producing "corruption and nepotism on a massive scale." For the nation to progress, Indians must "arrive at a consensus about the 'Idea' of India . . . recognize the power of its world-view," and "redesign our approach in consonance with the . . . preferences of the Indian people."[29]

The manifesto therefore stresses that India is a democracy, and the BJP has often treated it as a majoritarian democracy, in which the "civilizational consciousness" of its supermajority of Hindus should prevail. Still, the manifesto recognizes India as a "diverse country" in which different "communities settled in vastly different regions have their own aspirations." It promises a "highly decentralized federal structure" that will recognize the "special needs" and "unique status" of different regions and territories, in reticulated fashion. Nevertheless, it states, "all this should happen within the framework of our constitution and with the spirit of 'India First.' . . . Any activity, which disrupts the integrity of the nation, cannot be in the interest of any segment of the society or any region of the country." Insisting that the "BJP recognizes the importance of diversity in Indian society," it explains that "the party believes in the principle of unity in diversity." It maintains that this vision of India extends to "all . . . ethnic social and cultural groups," including the "Muslim community" now "stymied in poverty," because "our culture . . . is defined by tolerance and co-existence." The "only philosophy and religion of a Government," it concludes, "should be India First."[30]

Much of the document is devoted to proposals for sweeping improvements in democratic processes and public administration, and for pro-business economic development and educational initiatives. The Indian story of peoplehood told in the BJP's manifesto thus advances capitalist economic themes. It celebrates participatory democracy and reticulated, federal governance as the preferred ways to structure political power. It commits not just to respect for all cultural, religious, and regional communities, but to efforts to advance their progress.

These promises are in tension, however, with Manohar Joshi's denunciation of "alien" institutions as inferior to India's ancient "civilizational consciousness." The dominant narrative in the manifesto he wrote is again a mechanistic one, in which India can prosper only if it returns to the ancient civilization that once made India great. It is unclear how much diversity can survive this return—whether respect for multiculturalism, and especially the nation's Muslim minority, can really coexist with putting "India First." It is noteworthy that Joshi once faced prosecution for saying that if his party won a state election, it would create the "first Hindu state." The Indian Supreme Court eventually held this to be permissible political expression.[31]

It is also significant that Modi himself campaigned in 2014 primarily on promises to promote business-oriented economic development and to end political corruption, with less emphasis on Hindu nationalism than he had articulated in the past. Still, other BJP leaders have not been so reticent, before or since. Once in power, the BJP has banned cow slaughter for consumption, a policy that many see as responsible for a rise in lynchings of Muslims; appointed an outspoken Hindu nationalist monk, Yogi Adityanath, as chief minister in India's largest state, Uttar Pradesh; and authorized police measures officially to protect women that have permitted the frequent exercise of force against Muslim men. Despite the BJP's proclamations of respect for all religions, Adityanath has repeatedly made incendiary statements, such as castigating Mother Teresa for seeking to "Christianize" India. Most recently, the BJP government has ended the special status of the Muslim-majority state of Kashmir, a step many saw as an expression of Hindu nationalism. French political scientist Christophe Jaffrelot argues that under the BJP's leadership, "India is on the path to becoming an 'ethnic democracy,' " one that is majoritarian but not, in "the classical sense of the word, liberal."[32] Other observers believe that only "the Indian judiciary and the Election Commission of India" can check "India's continued majoritarian drift toward religious politics," and many despair of either institution doing so.[33] These analyses should make us question whether better stories of Indian peoplehood can curb the dangers of Hindu nationalist populism.

Still, the 2014 BJP platform professed no national religion other than "India First." It was not explicitly a call for India to be a Hindu nation. Modi most championed economic and infrastructure growth and criticized the antidemocratic continuation of traditional caste advantages, and the accompanying pervasive corruption, which the Congress Party, despite its similar rhetoric, had never eradicated.[34] The BJP won in 2014 by turning out large numbers of new voters, especially in urban areas, who were Hindu but disengaged from a political system they saw as closed and indifferent to them. In states where existing chief ministers had governed more effectively, incumbents retained strong electoral support.[35] Because just under 80 percent of Indians identify as Hindu, it is admittedly hard to disentangle majoritarianism from support for the idea of India as a Hindu nation. Yet it is not clear, despite the BJP's successes, that most Indians have ever embraced a "hard" Hindu nationalist view of Indian identity.[36]

The BJP's own manifesto confirms that Indian traditions and experiences also provide ingredients for very different and more inclusive stories of Indian peoplehood. As the distinguished political scientist Sunil Khilnani affirmed: "Those situated at different locations in Indian society have produced their own distinctive conceptions of the nation."[37] Until they were subject to British rule and British labeling, many diverse communities on the subcontinent did not even consider themselves Indian, though many shared "narrative structures embodied in epics, myths, and folk stories," as well as caste structures.[38] When they opposed British accounts of Indian identity with their own stories, they provided materials for many rival accounts of "who is an Indian?"[39]

Despite their variety, moreover, virtually all those stories converge on valorizing India as a democracy. Khilnani himself advanced a "grand narrative" in which "independent India appears as the third moment" in the "great democratic experiment launched . . . by the American and French revolutions." The key disputes among Indians have been over what sort of democracy is appropriate in light of India's extraordinary diversity. Mahatma Gandhi urged his nation to embrace a wide range of religious traditions, local beliefs, and identities within a shared "cultural consciousness," and he portrayed India as a land of diverse self-sustaining, democratic villages; but his highly spiritualist, strongly antistatist vision lost influence after independence.[40] Nonetheless, evocations persist to this day of an Indian prehistory of tolerant "village republics" as the authentic roots of Indian democracy.[41]

Jawaharlal Nehru, however, favored a strong democratic central state that would protect India's cultural and religious diversity by recognizing "interconnected differences," eventually including language-based states, all united behind socialist-leaning governmental initiatives for economic progress.[42] The great Dalit leader B. R. Ambedkar, influenced in part by his Columbia University mentor John Dewey, sought to promote a democratic society of fluid memberships and mobility. He believed, however, that in India this required a constitutional system guaranteeing distinctive economic, educational, and political opportunities to disadvantaged groups.[43] Under his influence, India's constitution and later policies created sets of group rights that generated material benefits and senses of membership in the state's democratic project; but these measures also fostered sharply conflicting political identities, movements, and parties. As the Congress Party faltered amid rising senses of division and fragmentation, many came to see Modi, the BJP, and Hindu nationalism ("Hindutva") as the best available option.[44]

Yet the nationalist Hindutva vision remains intensely controversial. In current debates on "the idea of India," many voices invoke the "founding idea of India . . . as a secular, pluralistic, and multicultural entity, all this wrapped in the idea of Democracy."[45] Whether they appeal to the constitution's recognition of diversity within a national democracy, Gandhi's diverse democratic villages, or even the BJP's narrative of India as providing "the most ennobling experience in spiritual co-existence" in a democratic federation, conceptions of India as a more pluralistic, reticulated democracy than is provided by simple majoritarianism appear to retain great resonance.[46] There may be real potential for a variety of stories that address economic and corruption concerns and persuasively depict India as a great modern democracy whose distinctive culture enables it to progress while accommodating, indeed celebrating, vast diversity. If these stories contend that India's special traditions and experiences actually make it the greatest of modern democratic nations, thereby raising fears of chauvinism, the political potency of this idea of India may still make it, on balance, beneficial.

With trepidation, I turn briefly to one last example: Israel. All too often, people judge everything one says about modern politics by what one has said about Israel. It also is not clear to what extent Israel's governing coalition is part of the current worldwide surge of right-wing nationalist populisms, though some of its partners clearly fit the bill.[47] Still, recent events have made Israel a perfect example of contrasting narratives of peoplehood.

As Meral Ugur Cinar and I have argued, many authoritative Israeli sources, like nationalist populists in other lands, have long told the story of their peoplehood as governed by an enduring law or mechanism. We have summed up that law as: "When Jews have a state of their own in the homeland of Israel, they prosper; when they do not have that state, they suffer." The 1948 Declaration of the Establishment of the State of

Israel, for example, depicted the "Land of Israel" as the original home of the Jewish people, where they "created cultural values of national and universal significance" before "being forcibly exiled from their land." After that, Jews "in every successive generation" sought to return home, until they were at last able to do so after the horrors of the Holocaust.[48] The Declaration and other founding documents of Israel famously presented it as both a "Jewish" and a "democratic" state, creating tensions and aspirations that have been central features of Israeli life ever since. The Declaration also made prominent commitments to respect all persons' basic rights and liberties. It said that Israel "will foster the development of the country for the benefit of all its inhabitants" and "ensure complete equality of social and political rights to all its inhabitants irrespective of religion, race, or sex" by providing "freedom of religion, conscience, language, education and culture." It called for "the Arab inhabitants of the State of Israel to preserve peace and participate in the upbuilding of the state on the basis of full and equal citizenship," even as it referred to "the sovereign Jewish people" now "settled in its own land."[49]

Though much has happened since 1948, the question of whether Israel can truly be both a Jewish state and a democracy that accords full and equal rights and citizenship to its Arab inhabitants has only grown more acute. On July 19, 2018, the Knesset approved a new Basic Law defining Israel as "the Nation State of the Jewish People." It reasserted that the "land of Israel is the national home of the Jewish People" and that the "State of Israel" fulfills that people's "natural, cultural, religious and historical right to self-determination." The Basic Law specifies that this right to "national self-determination in the State of Israel is unique to the Jewish people." It says the "state's language is Hebrew," though the "Arabic language has a special status in the state." "Non-Jews" also "have a right to maintain days of rest on their Sabbaths and festivals."[50] But the new Basic Law does not repeat the promises of "complete equality of social and political rights" and "full and equal citizenship" for Arab inhabitants made in the 1948 Declaration.

The new law therefore triggered many debates, including a striking one on the op-ed pages of the *New York Times.* On August 14, 2018, Ronald S. Lauder, president of the World Jewish Congress, published a column entitled "Israel, This Is Not Who We Are." Lauder wrote, "The nation-state law, which correctly reaffirms that Israel is a Jewish state . . . damages the sense of equality and belonging of Israel's Druze, Christian and Muslim citizens." Telling his own story of Jewish peoplehood, Lauder argued: "For 4,000 years the Jewish people were seen as the world's moral compass. The Zionist movement has been unwaveringly democratic from its very start. Writ large upon its flag were liberty, equality and human rights for all." And Israel's founding Declaration, Lauder noted, guaranteed equality of social and political rights as well as freedoms of religion, language, and culture. He maintained: "Theodor Herzl, Chaim Weismann, Zeev Jabotinsky, David Ben Gurion and Golda Meir always emphasized the need to combine Jewish nationalism with universal humanism." "For over 200 years," Lauder argued, "modern Judaism has aligned itself with enlightenment," fusing "national pride and religious affiliation with a dedication to human progress, worldly culture and morality." But in his view the new Basic Law and the current Israeli government were acting to "crush the core of contemporary Jewish existence." Lauder concluded that "This is not who we are, and this is not who we wish to be," and he called for efforts to "ensure that Israel will continue to be the Jewish democratic state it is meant to be."[51] If the Danes have the potential to tell their national story as one in which different communities partner ever more strongly in advancing the Danish welfare project, and if Indians have the potential to tell their story as one in which the world's largest democracy thrives while respecting and advancing many forms of diversity, Lauder suggests that Israelis can view themselves as the democracy that can show the world how to blend distinctive Jewish values and allegiances ever more fully over time with the best humanistic values of the Enlightenment. For him, that more teleologically structured narrative is a source of inspiration and pride.

But Naftali Bennett, Israel's minister of education, quickly fired off a response to Lauder, headlined "Israel Is Proud of Who We Are." He contended that the new Basic Law had passed "only after decades of successive rulings by Israel's judiciary that have ignored the aspirations of those who seek to preserve the Jewish nature of our state." In his view, the Israel Supreme Court's interpretations of another Basic Law, entitled "Human Dignity and Liberty," in cases involving "immigration and the extension of Israeli citizenship to Palestinians," amounted to "a direct attack on Israel's Jewish character." Bennett praised the government's "efforts to ensure equality in education, academia and employment for Israel's Arab communities," and he insisted that "Israel's other Basic Laws . . . reinforce the freedom of expression and equality for all citizens of Israel." He conceded that the Druze of Israel were "right to point out" that their "special relationship with the Jewish state" was not affirmed in the new Nation State Law, and he thought that should "be rectified—by means other than changing the law passed." That law had to stand, in order to keep "Israel as the Jewish nation-state."[52]

For liberals, Bennett's claim that equal citizenship for Arab Israelis is protected by the state's other Basic Laws, even as he attacked the Israel Supreme Court's rulings based on the Basic Law of Human Dignity and Liberty, was not persuasive. For conservatives, Lauder's claim that Israel's identity as a Jewish state was threatened by a law reaffirming that identity was even less convincing. My aim here is not to arbitrate this debate. Rather, I wish to highlight it as an example of how those who see themselves as proponents of universal values of democracy and human rights, as Lauder does, can tell a deeply contextual, particularist story of how their community's heritage, ethos, and spirit, its historical achievements and its modern commitments, all call for respecting and advancing those values.[53] It is also significant that Lauder is an American who leads an international advocacy organization for Jewish communities. The fact that he criticized Israel's new law in the *New York Times*, and that Education Minister Bennett felt compelled to respond immediately, shows how national efforts to define peoplehood today, especially in small, isolated nations like Israel but also in many other places, often face challenges from groups and movements beyond their borders they do not feel they can ignore.

In many places today, those kinds of challenges can be much more persuasive when connected criticism and advocacy inform the kind of stories of distinctive peoplehood that Ronald Lauder advanced. More persuasive does not, however, mean always victorious. It is highly unlikely that Israel will soon change its new national law, or any of the other recent measures that Lauder faulted. And if we look around the world for evidence that candidates offering inclusive, egalitarian, yet particularistic stories of peoplehood are able to defeat right-wing populists, there is not an abundance of current examples. Again, progressives in many lands shy away from advancing accounts of their political communities that might sound stridently nationalistic, or unduly celebratory of dominant groups. In any case, the major story of recent elections is undeniably the surge of success for right-wing populists, so accounts of surprising successes for other politicians of any sort are hard to find.

Yet there are some. In Peru, Jorge Muñoz Wells unexpectedly won election as mayor of Lima in October 2018 over several right-leaning national populist candidates, who may have divided their kindred voters, allowing Muñoz to squeak through: he received just 32.4 percent of the municipal vote.[54] Still, it is notable that the new mayor first came to prominence as a member of the Somos Peru (We Are Peru) party, leaving it when it partnered with the Allianza Para et Progresso (Alliance for Progress party), whose leader, César Acuña, had been accused of misuse of funds, domestic abuse, and other offenses.[55] As the candidate of the Acción Popular (Popular Action) party, Muñoz promised to "generate social transformations through a culture that considers difference a development opportunity" and to "generate conditions of equity and . . . participation" for "vulnerable groups."[56] He presented these goals as part of the vision of Lima and Peru he had long favored. In an election year when Brazil chose an extreme right-wing populist—in a jarring swing from previous presidential victories for left-wing candidates—it is notable that a candidate in Peru's largest city who openly championed an embrace of diversity as part of a progressive patriotic vision could win, even against a divided field.

Another example of an effort to build an anti-right populist movement around an inclusive vision of national identity is the Mindenki Magyarországa Mozgalom/MMM (Everybody's Hungary Movement, or the All-Hungarian Movement). The MMM was founded by Péter Márki-Zay, an independent and a political novice who in February 2018 won a stunning 57 percent of the vote in the mayoral by-election of Hódmezővásárhely, a city thought to be a stronghold of Viktor Orbán's Fidesz party.[57] The new movement was, to be sure, unable to prevent a massive victory for Orbán and Fidesz nationally in the ensuing April 2018 election, and Orbán immediately set about rewriting the nation's constitution to enhance his power.[58] Yet Márki-Zay and

MMM have continued to organize in opposition; and contrary to expectations, the movement has attracted participation from all the nation's major left-leaning as well as center-right parties.[59]

From the start, Márki-Zay has presented himself as conservative in his allegiance both to Hungary and to a "market economy." However, he has also indicated a willingness to support Socialists in regions where they are competitive with Fidesz. He champions restoration of "democracy, freedom of the press, the state of law . . . and the commitment to European integration."[60] At this writing it is far too soon to tell how often Márki-Zay's unexpected spring 2018 electoral success can be repeated, when a regime which Orbán has proudly proclaimed to be an "illiberal democracy" is clearly in the saddle. Yet it is still significant that this isolated electoral success against Fidesz came from a candidate who advanced a vision that was both nationalistic and inclusive, even receptive toward the "external reticulated community" of the European Union.

Still more striking, in June 2019, the candidate of President Erdoğan's Justice and Development Party lost for mayor of Istanbul, gaining less support in a repeat election than he had in a contest the previous March, which Erdoğan's party had challenged. The successful candidate, Ekrem Imamoğlu, had support from an alliance of opposition parties, united against Erdoğan's increasingly authoritarian governance and his responses to Turkey's recent recession. Imamoğlu promised to "build democracy" and "justice" in the city, and "to embrace everyone," saying no one's "lifestyle and how they dress is a concern for us."[61] The defeat of Erdoğan's candidate suggests that both his economic and democratic political power themes had lost credibility, belied by adverse events. But the Istanbul electorate supported disavowal of his narrow religious nationalism as well.

These victories remain rare and recent. We cannot know whether telling stories of political peoplehood that affirm pluralistic, egalitarian measures will succeed politically in Hungary, Turkey, or elsewhere on an enduring basis. Still, it is hard to see how, in the present moment, major successes can be won without them. The same is true, I submit, in the United States, to which we next turn.

3
Who Are We Americans Now?

The Need for American Stories

The late, highly accomplished and highly controversial political scientist Samuel P. Huntington entitled his last book *Who Are We? The Challenges to America's National Identity.*[1] In 2017, book critic Carlos Lozada called Huntington "a prophet for our time" because "his vision," especially as expressed in this book, is "partially reflected" in Donald Trump's "message and appeal," even though, Lozada said, Huntington might have been "apprehensive" about Trump's personal traits.[2] In *Who Are We?* Huntington not only departed from but subtly mocked his own earlier view that American identity rests strictly on embrace of the liberal democratic principles of the "American Creed."[3] To my surprise, he cited with approval my criticism of this view as "at best a half-truth."[4] The other half, Huntington now contended, was that American identity has a "cultural core," an "Anglo-Protestant culture" that he saw as threatened by "Mexican immigration" and "militant Islam."[5]

The similarities of Huntington's arguments to statements by Donald Trump, who began his presidential campaign by warning against Mexican immigration and later called for a ban on Muslim immigrants, are clear. Those two positions defined Trump as an anti-immigrant populist, much like many other right-wing populist leaders around the world today. Such ideas are anathema to those of us who believe America has benefited enormously from immigration, including Mexican and Muslim immigrants, and that the United States has deeply entrenched traditions of racial and religious as well as gender bigotry that must always be firmly combated, not championed.

Yet statements like these have helped Trump rise to heights few thought possible. Although most leaders of both parties not only opposed but openly ridiculed Trump early in 2016, he defied expectations, in part because he told a story of American peoplehood that resonated deeply with enough ordinary Americans to enable him to win the Republican presidential nomination easily, and then the electoral college vote narrowly. In his inaugural address, building on a decision made during his campaign, President Trump gave his story a name that echoed the successful manifesto of India's Hindu nationalist BJP. He promised: "From this day forward, a new vision will govern our land. From this day forward, it's going to be only America first. America first."[6]

In previous chapters I have argued that in many political contexts today, it is both possible and necessary to combat narrow, repressive stories of peoplehood with more inclusive, egalitarian ones. Is it necessary to advance such stories in America today, and if so, can better stories be found? My answer, unsurprisingly, is yes to both. To make that case, I will first consider President Trump's "America First" vision more fully, and then turn to some alternative accounts of American peoplehood that might constructively compete with it. I will explain why I regard one of these stories, portraying America as devoted to carrying forth the Declaration of Independence project of securing rights for all people everywhere, as on balance the best American story. My goal is not, however, to persuade everyone to accept it. Instead, my hope is to encourage others to put forth a variety of distinct though overlapping good stories of American peoplehood, enriching democratic discussions that should ultimately decide who we are as Americans now.

America First!

President Trump's inaugural address perfectly fit modern scholarship's minimalist definition of populism as an "ideology that posits a struggle between the will of the common people and a conspiring elite."[7] It also fit the mechanistic structure, depicting an iron law of the need for the people to rule, that is common in nationalist populist narratives today. Trump related the tale of America's past as one in which "a small group in our nation's Capital has reaped the rewards of government" while "the people have borne the cost. . . . Too many of our citizens" have experienced "American carnage." But, he announced, "January 20, 2017, will be remembered as the day the people became the rulers of this nation again." That restoration of popular power was what was needed today, what was always needed, to make America great. This was Trump's central theme concerning political power, though he also promised greater protection against violent crime and a stronger military for the nation.

Regarding economic concerns, the president promised a future in which every "decision on trade, on taxes, on immigration, on foreign affairs, will be made to benefit American workers and American families." New initiatives, he proclaimed, would "bring back our jobs . . . bring back our borders . . . bring back our wealth," with "new roads, and highways, and bridges, and airports, and tunnels, and railways." Through all this and more, he would get people "off of welfare and back to work," and that, too, would "make America great again."[8]

Above all, President Trump emphasized his core constitutive theme of the American people's inherent, though now violated, greatness. He did not, to be sure, repeat his campaign statement that "our American culture is the best in the world."[9] His America First vision, Trump explained, rested on the conviction that "a nation exists to serve its citizens. . . . It is the right of all nations to put their own nation first." So America First was a philosophy Trump suggested all nations could and should emulate; but whether or not they did so was strictly their choice. Americans, Trump maintained, "do not seek to impose our way of life on anyone, but rather to let it shine as an example for everyone to follow." He also contended that his vision encompasses "all the citizens of America." Americans, he said, form "one nation," sharing "one heart, one home, and one glorious destiny," with "no room for prejudice." Instead, all Americans should know "that whether we are black or brown or white, we all bleed the same red blood of patriots." Then, in a manner that many proponents of diversity found ominous, Trump asserted, "The bedrock of our politics will be a total allegiance to the United States of America, and through our loyalty to our country, we will rediscover our loyalty to each other."[10]

In terms of the three criteria for good stories of peoplehood outlined in the previous chapter, Trump's America First narrative certainly resonated with economic, cultural, and political concerns and deeply valued identities of many millions of Americans. He also sought to convey respect for all American citizens as well as for other nations. But his vision of America appeared to leave little room for reticulation, for the greatest feasible recognition and accommodation of the many diverse communities, cultures, and ways of life that constitute modern America. His rhetoric raised worries that, in a pluralistic society, demands for "total allegiance" might lead to totalitarian consequences.[11]

Before and since his inauguration, Trump's tweets, speeches, and most important his policies have provided abundant evidence of his hostility to many forms of diversity. In the years before he declared his candidacy, Trump's repeated challenges to Barack Obama's citizenship already suggested that he found something "un-American" about an African-American president. During the campaign, he contended that an American-born judge of Mexican descent could not apply the law fairly, and he disparaged the lives of black and brown Americans, grossly overstating criminal statistics for blacks and immigrants.[12] At a May 2016 rally, Trump reportedly said, "The only important thing is the unification of the people—because the other people don't mean anything."[13]

Whatever personal racial views Trump holds, moreover, his promises to "Make America Great Again" clearly spoke most powerfully to those who looked back favorably on an older, predominantly white Christian male-governed nation. Analysts of his electoral support overwhelmingly concur that Americans who believe that the United States should be a predominantly European-descended Christian nation saw Trump as their candidate. John Sides, writing as part of the Democracy Fund Voter Study Group, found that in the summer of 2016, 30 percent of Trump supporters thought it was important for Americans to be of European ancestry; 72 percent thought Americans should be born in the United States; and 63 percent thought being Christian was fairly or very important to being American.[14] These figures, all much higher than those for any other candidate, led Lynn Vavreck to conclude: "Mr. Trump's focus on ethnicity, religion, and American identity was the catalyst that united a relatively small set of Republican primary voters behind him and helped him defy expectations and become the G.O.P. nominee."[15]

In office, Trump's comments contending that there were "very good people" among the white supremacist protestors at

Charlottesville, criticizing African-American athletes and celebrities protesting police violence against people of color, reportedly derogating African countries and Haitian immigrants, and more have continued to appeal to those with strong senses of white identity, while alienating other Americans.[16] Moreover, Trump and his appointees have done much to advance these voters' social policy preferences, though promised economic initiatives to build roads, highways, bridges, airports, tunnels, and railways have not happened. Under Attorney General Jefferson Sessions and his successors, the Justice Department's Civil Rights Division has pursued lawsuits against universities suspected of overemphasizing race in their affirmative-action admissions policies.[17] The Justice Department and the Department of Housing and Urban Development, headed by Ben Carson, have stopped filing disparate impact suits to advance the Fair Housing Act's goal of fighting racial discrimination in housing.[18] The Trump administration also quietly ended a federal grant to a group working to oppose white nationalist extremist organizations.[19] It created a commission to investigate vote fraud led by one of the nation's most extreme proponents of anti-immigrant and voter restriction laws, Kansas Secretary of State Kris Kobach.[20] The commission faltered, but administration and Republican support for voter initiatives that are likely to suppress nonwhite voting continued.

Sessions and former Trump adviser Steve Bannon have each praised the race-based National Origins Quota system that governed immigration to the United States from the 1920s through 1965.[21] Though there are no plans to revive it, the administration sought to add a citizenship question to the census that could aid deportations—suspending the effort only when the Supreme Court challenged the administration's rationale for it—and it has favored immigration legislation that would replace family unification priorities fostering demographic diversity with preferences for high-skilled immigrants, and perhaps reduce overall legal immigration.[22] Leading up to the 2018 midterm elections, Trump stoked fears about a caravan of impoverished Central Americans moving toward the Mexican-American border, and he deployed thousands of troops to guard against the alleged threat. He contended that Democrats supported immigrant murderers, and he threatened to issue a clearly unconstitutional executive order depriving children of unauthorized alien parents of birthright citizenship.[23]

These policies and statements, along with many more, make it difficult to see Trump's America First program as genuinely respectful toward and responsive to all Americans, or even as clearly committed to democracy, human rights, and the rule of law. Americans therefore have a civic and moral duty to explore whether there are better stories of American peoplehood that might check these features of Trump's America First vision, while also responding to the legitimate concerns to which he has spoken powerfully.

There are many candidates. Ronald Reagan loved to tell the story of America as a nation chosen to be a shining "city on a hill," and George W. Bush built on that theme to contend that America was "called to lead the cause of freedom" as part of its "mission to promote liberty around the world."[24] Daniel Rodgers has shown that John Winthrop's original lay sermon was primarily a call to build "a community rooted in love" to soften the tensions of what Winthrop saw as inevitable social inequality, and also a warning that people should live as if the "moral scrutiny of the world" was upon them. It was far from the celebration of capitalism it became for Reagan, or the call to a global crusade that it became for Bush.[25] Still, it is in the nature of these stories that they can be reinterpreted for many purposes. That is why they can help to build shared senses of community and continuity over time. Many Americans today continue to find hope and inspiration in understanding America as a "city on a hill."

Yet from the standpoint of the three criteria for good stories of peoplehood I have advanced, this narrative of the nation's Puritan forebears has serious limitations. Winthrop's vision was of a religiously homogenous theocracy, one guided by a teleological organic narrative of community purpose that was understood to be imposed by a demanding Protestant Christian God, who would have no other gods before him. Despite its call for the Massachusetts colony to be a "model of Christian charity," Winthrop's view had little room for any deep and broad acceptance of diversity. As governor, Winthrop contended, against calls to welcome those who dissented from Puritan beliefs, that "a commonwealth is a great family," but that just "as a family is not bound to entertain all comers, no not every good man (otherwise than by way of hospitality) no more is a commonwealth."[26] So Winthrop opposed accepting many immigrants, and he helped drive religious dissenters out of Massachusetts, including Roger Williams and Anne Hutchinson, who have since become icons of American spiritual freedom.[27]

George W. Bush's similar understanding of the American story was one in which, as he put it in his eloquent first inaugural address, "an angel . . . rides in the whirlwind and directs this storm."[28] But when Bush used this narrative to justify repeated U.S. military actions around the world, with dire unintended consequences, his example convinced many Americans, including Donald Trump, that the United States should seek to be an isolationist-leaning model, rather than a perennially intervening crusader nation. Bush's Protestant-inflected providentialist story fostered policies that failed to respect the rights of many outside the United States, even as they professed to seek to secure those rights.

I do not feel entitled to judge President Bush too harshly. In an all too similar fashion, I previously suggested that Americans should see themselves as "a pioneering people," constantly in quest of bold, creative innovations that can improve the quality of human lives.[29] Although I still see much of value in the pioneering spirit that has played so prominent a role in America's development, it is evident in the twenty-first century that this pioneering theme is too deeply entangled with the long, dark history of U.S. and European imperialism to serve as a desirable story of American peoplehood now. Those who fear that all stories of national identity can easily be put to bad purposes are far from foolish.

The United States has, however, other and better options available to it. In terms of the criteria I have offered, there are three narratives of American identity that are particularly promising. These are, first, American politics as a democratic project, the view of John Dewey and others; second, America as a constitutional endeavor seeking a more perfect union, without effacing diversity, the *e pluribus unum* story told best by Barack Obama; and third, America defined by the Declaration of Independence project of extending rights to all, the vision articulated most memorably by Abraham Lincoln.

All three of these stories can be structured as teleological narratives of organic growth, aimed respectively at greater and greater democracy; greater and greater unity, while preserving inclusive diversity; and greater and greater enjoyment of basic rights. But these are far more open teleologies than Winthrop's "city on a hill" account. Each, especially democratic narratives, can be seen as calling chiefly for contextual adaptations to alleviate the felt problems of the day in ways that move the country in the right direction, rather than as an appeal to drive immediately and single-mindedly toward a distant end. And all are narratives in which progress must come, if it comes at all, not primarily through the agency of providence or the playing out of iron laws of history, but rather through the self-defining choices and actions of the people themselves. Individually and at times in concert, each story can guide Americans toward the difficult recognition that all political peoples need to accept today—that who we are inescapably rests, in large part, on who we decide we should be.

Democratic Stories

As is well known, many of the framers of the American Constitution, including James Madison himself, harbored deep fears about the dangers of democracy and insisted that they were creating republics, governed by elected representatives rather than by direct popular rule.[30] Their embrace of popular self-governance, however, proved difficult to cabin. With fits, starts, some important reversals, and continuing battles today, the history of the United States displays progressively wider and deeper embraces of democracy. These steps include renaming the party of Jefferson as the Democratic Party in the age of Jackson; the expansion of the franchise to all white men, then all men, then all male and female citizens twenty-one and over, and eventually eighteen-year-olds as well; the adoption of direct election of judges in many states in the nineteenth century and of U.S. senators via the 17th Amendment; and the democratization of candidate selection processes through the spread of primaries in the twentieth century. These historical developments suggest that stories of America as a democratic project have a serious claim to be the accounts that have best advanced inclusive, egalitarian visions of American peoplehood in the past. They also may be the best to do so today.

Commitments to democracy in fact suggest an important alternative to the whole strategy of developing good stories of peoplehood that I am proposing here. It is possible that egalitarian inclusion is most attainable through promoting broad, often grassroots democratic engagement in self-governance, without advancing any particular account of just who "the people" are. Perhaps organizing around resistance to specific forms of oppression, exploitation, and domination in the name of achieving more democratic and egalitarian conditions is sufficient, and safer. America's greatest democratic theorist, John Dewey, often argued in this vein. His books, articles, and speeches frequently focused on the need to combat democracy-distorting economic inequalities and concentrations of corporate power, and to expand participatory democratic decision making, sometimes transnationally, rather than on any tale of America's distinctive identity. He was repelled by the chauvinistic ethnic nationalism of the World War I era that conceived of America as "Anglo-saxondom."[31] More recently, in calling for a "left populism" aimed at mobilizing mass power and opposing pro-business neoliberal economic policies, the European political theorist Chantal Mouffe has acknowledged the risk that "to bring together . . . democratic demands in the creation of a 'people' will produce"—or worse, presume—"a homogeneous subject, one that negates plurality."[32]

But as Dewey sometimes did and as I have done here, Mouffe argues that democratic projects must "be congruent with the values and identities" of those they seek to join in support of common causes.[33] They must start from where people "are and how they feel, offering them a vision of the future that gives them hope."[34] At our current historical juncture, Mouffe contends, this often means beginning "at the national level" and mobilizing people "around a patriotic identification with the best and most egalitarian aspects of the national tradition."[35] She does not go so far as to argue that we must develop better stories of peoplehood or to suggest how that might be done, but her analysis points in that direction. Mouffe stops short precisely because, like Dewey, she wants notions of "the people" to be constructed "around democracy," with "democratic values in the leading role" in defining political identities everywhere—not distinctive accounts of peoplehood.[36]

This endeavor is worth pursuing. Still, there are reasons to doubt whether single-minded devotion to democracy as the central goal of political life can provide a sufficient sense of common purpose to play the mobilizing role asked of it. In this regard, sociologist Ruth Braunstein's 2017 book, *Prophets and Patriots: Faith in Democracy across the Political Divide,* is instructive.[37] Beginning in 2010, Braunstein engaged in extensive ethnographic observations and discussions with members of a liberal religious activist group, called Interfaith, and a Tea Party group called the Patriots. She found that, although these groups differed sharply on many issues and organized in different ways, they shared some common grievances and some common ideals. They embraced a "similar ideal of good citizenship," which they understood to mean active engagement in furthering the American democratic project.[38] In this Braunstein very reasonably found some hope. She argued, much as I have done, that as long as "multiple groups cultivate and enact different stories of America, and no single story becomes dominant," their commitments to democratic engagement might lead them to search for enough common ground and to accept enough compromises to hold the nation together and even enable it to progress.[39]

Braunstein also noted, however, that despite their overlapping senses of commitment to the project of American democracy, her two groups had fundamental disagreements on a number of economic and cultural issues that appeared "nearly impossible to resolve."[40] It is not clear whether even the strong and shared senses of these groups that they are dedicated to advancing democracy can enable them to work together constructively. The very activism of Braunstein's prophets and patriots, moreover, probably indicates that they are more drawn to democratic engagement than most Americans are. It is true that civic republican and more modern democratic traditions valorizing active public service are significant features of American political culture. But most Americans probably see democratic activism the way that Oscar Wilde famously described socialism: it takes up too many of one's evenings.

Efforts to motivate an inclusive, egalitarian politics solely through appeals to democracy face other challenges as well. As the history of the United States and many other countries shows, if democracy means unqualified majoritarian rule, the rights of many religious, ethnic, and cultural minorities are not likely to be safe. In addition, as James Madison warned and as Frances Rosenbluth and Ian Shapiro have recently affirmed, many institutions, such as the selection of representatives, can be excessively or at least poorly democratized. Malfunctioning democratic institutions can make it necessary to save "democracy from itself," in Rosenbluth and Shapiro's words, or to find a "republican remedy for the diseases most incident to republican government," in the words of Madison.[41]

Perhaps most disturbingly, fewer than half of young Americans today say they take an active interest in politics. They also are less inclined than older Americans to affirm democracy as always the best form of government.[42] A citizenry that is disengaged from politics and disillusioned with democracy is not likely to be roused by stories of peoplehood that feature democracy above all else. There are, in sum, serious obstacles to seeking to make democratic values the central theme of American political life. To be sure, all options face obstacles. Still, these considerations suggest that in addition to stories of Americans as a people engaged in democratic self-governance, movements to defeat pathological forms of populism in the United States will benefit from additional stories of American peoplehood.

THE E PLURIBUS UNUM STORY

The preamble to the Constitution summarizes the purposes for which "We the People of the United States" created our federal government. The first goal was "to form a more perfect Union." Soon thereafter, in 1789, Congress adopted the Great Seal of the United States with a design that included the motto "E Pluribus Unum"—out of many, one. Since the nation's founding, then, it has always been possible to narrate the American people as devoted to forming a greater unity out of their manifold diversity. Yet no American political leader has ever identified the American story and his own story so fully with that goal as Barack Obama did, beginning with the speech at the 2004 Democratic Convention that catapulted him to prominence. There Obama expressed gratitude "for the diversity of my heritage," and he stressed that his biography was "part of the larger American story" in ways that made him indebted to the USA. In "no other country on earth," Obama avowed, could his story be "even possible."[43] Obama traced that possibility back to America's commitment to the proposition in the Declaration of Independence that all "are created equal." But he did not contend that the American project was simply or chiefly to secure equal rights for all. Instead, using biblical and familial language, he maintained that "alongside our famous individualism, there's another ingredient in the American saga, a belief that we're all connected as one people. . . . I am my brother's keeper, I am my sister's keeper. . . . It's what allows us to pursue our individual dreams and yet still come together as one American family. E pluribus unum: 'Out of many, one.' "[44]

The larger story of America that Obama portrayed appealed to the Declaration of Independence, but interpreted it in light of the nation's religious traditions of moral obligation as well as republican conceptions of civic virtues and duties. In the 2007 speech in which he announced his candidacy for the presidency, Obama said his campaign was "about reclaiming the meaning of citizenship, restoring our sense of common purpose."[45] When his campaign faced a crisis due to inflammatory remarks by his pastor, Reverend Jeremiah Wright, Obama responded with a speech at the National Constitution Center in Philadelphia that began by describing the Constitution as "stained by this nation's original sin of slavery," but with "the answer to the slavery question" already "embedded" in it. The Constitution, according to Obama, "had at its very core the ideal of equal citizenship under the law." It "promised its people liberty, and justice, and a union that could be and should be perfected over time." To continue in that quest, Obama asserted, Americans needed to see "that we may have different stories, but we hold common hopes. . . . We all want to move in the same direction," defined by "the idea that . . . out of many, we are truly one."[46]

In a speech at Cairo in 2009, Obama restated his claim that America was "shaped by every culture, drawn from every end of the Earth, and dedicated to a simple concept: E pluribus unum—'Out of many, one.' " He affirmed that this was a cosmopolitan aim, asserting that globally as well as domestically, all people have a "responsibility . . . to one another as human beings" to work together for common benefit.[47] Speaking to his fellow Americans in his 2012 nomination acceptance speech, Obama maintained that the nation's founding beliefs in inalienable rights fostered commitments to "personal responsibility" and "individual initiative," but also to "citizenship . . . the idea that this country only works when we accept certain obligations to one another and to future generations."[48] And in his stirring second inaugural, Obama called the Declaration's self-evident truths of human equality and inalienable rights "what makes us Americans," while insisting that "preserving our individual freedoms ultimately requires collective action . . . as one nation and one people . . . as citizens."[49]

Obama's remarkable success in becoming the nation's first African-American president and then winning reelection proves that this story, especially in his telling, had undeniable resonance. It promised respect for all in ways that pointed to recognition of many forms of legitimate, indeed valuable diversity. It thus complied with the three Rs of good stories of peoplehood. It also seamlessly blended its constitutive theme of seeking unity without effacing diversity with calls for economic policies that would expand opportunities for all, and political power themes of ensuring voting rights for all and promoting democratic civic decision making.

Nonetheless, the experience of Obama's presidency raises cautions that Obama himself came to express. I have argued that he conceived of the American quest for "e pluribus unum" as best pursued in the spirit of John Dewey's democratic pragmatism and modern theories of deliberative democracy.[50] Even as Obama stressed that most forms of diversity need not and should not be suppressed in an effort to achieve a more perfect union, his openness to whatever economic and social policy solutions emerged from pragmatic deliberative democratic processes meant that his vision of union could appear devoid of any specific content—and therefore somewhat hollow. Still more important, when Republicans in Congress refused to engage in good-faith deliberations and negotiations over either legislation or presidential appointments, striving to make Obama's presidency fail, his "e pluribus unum" conception of the American project gave him no real guidance on how to respond. His best hope was simply to defeat his intransigent opponents at the polls. But while Obama remained popular, he did not find a way to sustain, much less expand, the broad base of support for his party he had built in 2008.

During his reelection campaign in 2012, Obama said that "the mistake of my first term" was "thinking that this job was just about getting the policy right. . . . The nature of this office is to tell a story to the American people that gives them a sense of unity and purpose and optimism, especially during tough times."[51] His second inaugural address told his "e pluribus unum" story perhaps as well as anyone has ever done; but it did not alter the reality of a nation that was growing more polarized, not more united. His foreign policy adviser and speechwriter Ben Rhodes has written that late in his second term, Obama read Yuval Harari's *Sapiens* and was reinforced in the belief that his job was to "tell a really good story about who we are."[52] At Hiroshima in May 2016, Obama reflected that nations "arise, telling a story that binds people together in sacrifice and cooperation . . . but those same stories have so often been used to oppress and dehumanize those who are different." He said, "My own nation's story began with simple words: All men are created equal, and endowed by our Creator with certain unalienable rights, including life, liberty, and the pursuit of happiness. Realizing that ideal has never been easy. . . . But staying true to that story is worth the effort."[53]

This time, however, Obama did not identify the American story with the quest to achieve "e pluribus unum," though he did insist that "the radical and necessary notion that we are part of a single human family—that is the story that we all must tell."[54] He seemed to acknowledge tacitly that American peoplehood should perhaps be defined by a different narrative than the one he had provided during the preceding dozen years. If Obama had indeed reached that conclusion, I believe he was correct.

THE DECLARATION OF INDEPENDENCE STORY

When Obama said at Hiroshima that his nation's story began with the words of the Declaration of Independence, he was advancing a view that has long been debated in America. Again, Ronald Reagan identified the nation's origins with John Winthrop's "City upon a Hill" sermon, while many antebellum Protestant Whigs like Daniel Webster traced the country back to the Plymouth colony.[55] Many scholars instead think of the adoption of the Constitution, not the Declaration, as the origin of America's national government. Not only critics of the Declaration, but also many American judges, have insisted that this "second founding" is the true, legally authoritative one.[56] The many Americans who have seen dangers in taking the universalistic, egalitarian language of the Declaration's opening too seriously, from antebellum southern slaveholders to Gilded Age proponents of a rule of law focused on property rights to some modern constitutional originalists, have mostly preferred to start their American stories in Philadelphia in 1787.

The most influential expression of the view that America instead began with the Declaration is Lincoln's Gettysburg Address in 1863, with its famous opening: "Fourscore and seven years ago, our fathers brought forth upon this continent a new nation, conceived in Liberty, and dedicated to the proposition that all men are created equal."[57] If we do the math or recognize the last five words, we know he is referring to 1776 and the Declaration of Independence. Lincoln arrived at this view of the nation's starting point well before Gettysburg, but he did not originate it. Lincoln also did not interpret its implications as Barack Obama would do, as a mandate to pursue "e pluribus unum," greater unity without effacing diversity.

Instead, Lincoln spoke in a broad American tradition of invoking the Declaration in order to claim that the nation's highest goal should be to secure the basic rights of more and more people, and eventually all people. By 1863 that tradition already included Jacksonian workers' advocates and the antebellum women's rights movement, and it has gone on to include champions of property rights, human rights, civil rights, LGBTQ rights, disability rights, and other rights, up to the present day.[58] Lincoln spoke particularly in the tradition of, though not in full agreement with, the advocates of antislavery constitutionalism, including the Massachusetts abolitionist Lysander Spooner and the editor and former slave Frederick Douglass.[59] In his 1845 book *The Unconstitutionality of Slavery,* Spooner argued that the "people of this country" first "announced their independent political existence" in a document, the Declaration, that amounted to "constitutional law," and that took as a "self-evident truth" that all men had a natural right to liberty. This moral principle, he insisted, made slavery unconstitutional—a position the 1787 Constitution did not, in Spooner's view, disavow.[60] Douglass, building on Spooner, came to argue—after breaking with the Garrisonian abolitionists, who saw the Constitution as enshrining slavery—that the courts, including the Supreme Court, regularly held that "the language of the law must be construed strictly in favour of justice and liberty" whenever legal texts so permitted.[61] Since the Constitution did not use the word "slavery" and explicitly promised, like the Declaration, to secure "the blessings of liberty," Douglass maintained that Americans could and should read it as an antislavery document.

Lincoln did not agree that the Constitution by itself banned slavery. Still, in the 1850s and 1860s, he and the new Republican Party came to adopt a moderate version of antislavery constitutionalism. They contended that the Constitution had been meant, and should be administered, to pursue the fulfillment of the principles of the Declaration by putting slavery on the path to preferably peaceful, gradual, but ultimately complete extinction.[62] In speeches throughout the 1850s,

Lincoln often called the Declaration's proclamation of human equality and inalienable rights a "maxim" set up for "future use." It should be "constantly looked to, constantly labored for, and even though never perfectly attained, constantly approximated," and so "constantly spreading and deepening its influence," thereby "augmenting the happiness and value of life to all people, of all colors, everywhere."[63]

Lincoln's embrace of the Declaration as the foundation of his political beliefs and his story of America shaped his economic themes, which called for national measures to promote economic opportunities while protecting property rights, the platform of the Whig Party to which Lincoln belonged until its demise. The Declaration also undergirded his steadfast commitment to structuring political power in systems of republican self-governance. And more than many critics appreciate, Lincoln's dedication to the Declaration's goals also propelled him through significant personal growth on racial issues. Though he had earlier urged only that African Americans deserved equality in regard to the basic rights of the Declaration of Independence, not full political equality, Lincoln eventually concluded that if African Americans were to gain meaningful possession of even those basic rights, many of them would need the franchise. It was his announcement of that position that spurred his assassination by John Wilkes Booth.

Lincoln's evolution on the question of African-American voting rights highlights a fundamental difference between his understanding of American peoplehood as a project of fulfilling the principles of the Declaration of Independence and Barack Obama's. For Obama, the goal was fostering unity through processes of deliberative democracy. If unity did not emerge, it was not clear what to do. For Lincoln, the goal was more specific and less conciliatory: the extension of basic rights to all, a project that policies *must* advance, and a project that could justify overriding, sometimes by force, the preferences of those who would deny rights to some.[64]

Lincoln's conception of American peoplehood contrasts far more sharply, however, with Trump's vision of America First. To be sure, Lincoln cast America's quest more as a means to make the nation a shining example to the world than a call to any active American interventions beyond our borders. Lincoln's focus was on holding the nation together. Lincoln was also a bitter opponent of the Mexican-American War that did so much to expand the nation's territories, seeing it as unjust and imperialistic. Yet when Lincoln said the nation should labor to spread the influence of the Declaration of Independence to augment the happiness and value of life for all people, there is no doubt that he meant all people. Unlike Trump, he never suggested there were "other people" who didn't matter.

Clear evidence of Lincoln's commitments in this regard came during the 1850s, at the height of the popularity of the anti-immigration Know-Nothings. Lincoln wrote then to his friend Joshua Speed, "I am not a Know-Nothing. That is certain. How could I be? How could anyone who abhors the oppression of negroes, be in favor of degrading classes of white people? Our progress in degeneracy appears to me to be pretty rapid. As a nation, we began by declaring that 'all men are created equal.' We now practically read it 'all men are created equal, except negroes.' When the Know-Nothings get control, it will read 'all men are created equal, except negroes, and foreigners, and catholics.' " If he were writing today, Lincoln might well add Mexicans and Muslims.[65] Though Lincoln was first and foremost concerned about his countrymen, he clearly thought that if any policies worked against the goal of securing the Declaration of Independence rights of all people of all colors everywhere, those policies violated the values to which the American people were and should be dedicated.

THE DECLARATION OF INDEPENDENCE STORY TODAY

Whether or not Lincoln and the Republicans were right to see the original Constitution as dedicated to the Declaration of Independence project of securing rights for all, they wrote their vision into the Constitution in the form of the three great Civil War amendments. The Declaration's principles can now clearly claim constitutional authority. That development is of fundamental importance, not only for the question of whether the goals of the Declaration of Independence can plausibly be placed at the center of stories of American peoplehood, but also for the broader question of how a nation can put principles of democracy and human rights in the core of its identity, yet still retain the conviction that its identity is distinctive and distinctively valuable. The tension between pledging allegiance to a civic identity grounded strictly on tenets of liberal democracy that purport to be universal, and simultaneously embracing a more particular conception of nationality, is, again, one that the standard liberal democratic responses to the challenges of pathological populism fail to address clearly or effectively. Does a story of American peoplehood as dedicated to realizing the goals of the Declaration of Independence do any better?

I believe it does. Admittedly, the Declaration describes the purpose of all legitimate governments as the securing of inalienable rights, without indicating that Americans and their governments have any exceptional role in this work. Yet its very existence allows Americans to claim a special status and identity. They can truthfully say theirs was the first nation to be explicitly "so conceived, and so dedicated," making it the original test case for this vision of political community and governance, as Lincoln said at Gettysburg. Seized by this vision, they replaced monarchy, aristocracy, and eventually theocracy, the dominant forms of governance in the European world and their own past, with a remarkable array of novel political and social institutions that in many regards remain distinctive, even as they have had global influence. Americans can and should also emphasize that they have struggled mightily with one another over the eradication of their most massive violation of their own stated principles, chattel slavery, making issues of race and region central and pervasive in their national experience, to a degree that citizens of other modern liberal democratic nations often have difficulty understanding.

All this makes it easy for Americans to see themselves as a people with a special historical role, distinctive achievements, and some very particular if not unique challenges in seeking to advance the aims of government set forth in the Declaration of Independence. They can see their national identity as resting not only on pledges to liberal democratic principles, but on being participants in a grand collective endeavor with a past, present, and future that are in important respects not like that of any other political community. Many therefore can and do find meaning not only through being dedicated to rights and democracy, but through being Americans. They are the offspring of the endeavors begun by the Declaration and the Constitution, and they are the prime beneficiaries, trustees, and sometimes victims of the resulting American way of life.

This sense of American identity has long resonated powerfully with an impressively wide range of the country's inhabitants, even as it has also inspired others around the world. Long before the Declaration of Independence's principles came to be more unequivocally lodged in the Constitution via the post–Civil War amendments, and to an even greater degree since, so many diverse movements have chosen to invoke the Declaration's principles that its story, like democratic stories, must be seen as a major historical asset for inclusive, egalitarian reforms, even though the wealthy have also used it to buttress their economic privileges.[66] Part of its resonance comes precisely from the support it can give to very different pursuits of happiness, rather than any single vision of human fulfillment, unlike particular religious views or even espousals of the centrality of democratic engagement to personal and community growth. Consequently, I believe this sense of American identity as dedicated to the Declaration of Independence's vision of securing rights for all links the principles of liberal democracy to a distinctive conception of American peoplehood more fully and effectively than standard accounts of "civic" national identities. It also provides a more broadly appealing and sustaining sense of purpose than either democratic stories or Obama's "e pluribus unum" story.

Still, to many ears, this narrative of American identity sounds many alarms. It may appear to be an effort to resuscitate eighteenth-century doctrines of natural rights that are now widely seen as intellectually discredited and politically pernicious, tied to narrow Christian and early Enlightenment notions of morality, and often employed to justify European and American imperialism. This Declaration of Independence story may also lead Americans to be obsessed with claiming rights for themselves as individuals, instead of pursuing common goods. Or Americans may rest satisfied with a formal equality of rights that belies the reality that many live in conditions of crippling material inequality. Worst of all, more privileged Americans or well-organized groups may use rights defined as they wish to impose their own self-interested conceptions of how others should live on diverse communities at home, as well as abroad.

These concerns have force. They suggest that collectively, Americans must rest their embrace of the Declaration of Independence's goals at least as much on modern pragmatic philosophic conceptions of rights as humanly crafted tools to achieve human goods, as on conceptions of rights as moral trumps, given that status by reason, nature, God, or perhaps the philosopher Immanuel Kant. There is no need, to be sure, to insist that all Americans must share the same foundational philosophic or religious commitments in regard to the sources and contents of rights. Some can be pragmatists, some can be Kantians, some can be traditionally religious, and many can hold many other beliefs. It is sufficient to search for areas of overlapping agreement. But there must be a practical willingness to accept overlapping agreement when it exists, rather than maintaining that the rights Americans seek to secure can be conceived of only in exactly the ways that those who adopted the Declaration and the Constitution conceived of them, or that some groups today conceive of them. Americans should accept as partners in their nation's Declaration of Independence project all those who embrace it, whether they rest their acceptance on worldviews prevalent in the twenty-first, twentieth, nineteenth, or eighteenth century, or indeed in ancient times, or in the global East and South as well as the North and West.

At the same time, because we are seeking a healthy politics for the twenty-first century, it is necessary to expand significantly upon the Civil War Republicans' understanding of what is involved in seeking to secure rights for all. As the intertwined history of labor and civil rights struggles has long affirmed, policies and practices must help people acquire the economic, educational, and political resources and capabilities they need to exercise their rights. Parchment guarantees are not enough (they have never been enough). Today in the United States as elsewhere, it is vital to find and adopt policies that can effectively address the needs and concerns of both the deeply disadvantaged and those constituencies who, though better off, still have reason to feel endangered by globalizing trends.

Americans disagree sharply about how to do this, particularly in regard to redistributive measures, public investments, and direct public provision of services. Lincoln favored state investment in "public roads and highways, public schools, charities," and "orphanages," as well as the administration of criminal and civil justice, along with all other things that people "cannot do, *at all,* or cannot, *so well do,* for themselves."[67] Today, his list goes too far for some. Still, most Americans appear willing to support some forms of national aid to communities and workers that lose jobs due to economic globalization or necessary environmental regulations. Many now recognize that the benefits of immigration tend to be national but the burdens are often locally concentrated, making it appropriate to adopt assistance programs for regions facing demands for expanded social services from very recent immigrants. Trade agreements that require better pay for workers in immigrant-sending regions, thereby reducing incentives to immigrate, can help answer both economic and cultural concerns about immigration. To his credit, Trump has sought them, though in erratic fashion. A still greater opportunity, however, is the America First promise Trump has neglected: public infrastructure spending on transportation, communications, energy production, water supply, and educational facilities, with environmental protections. These investments could generate immediate employment for many displaced native workers who supported Trump, and for the immigrants he has assailed, while spurring sustained economic growth that would generate still more jobs for decades to come.

As Lincoln eventually recognized in regard to the nation's African-American citizens, it is also a continuing task for Americans to improve their democratic institutions, certainly by removing instead of imposing barriers to participation, perhaps by altering candidate selection processes to reduce the influence of extremist activists. Most important now is to make Congress the centerpiece of representative governance that it was meant to be, and for many decades actually was, before heightened electoral preoccupations and polarization led it to cede authority to the other branches.[68]

It is, moreover, simply true that powerful groups have often prompted American governments to impose those groups' preferred forms of economic activities, religious practices, and cultural life on many minorities at home, and on other political societies abroad. These practices violate the Declaration of Independence project, for its rights include liberty and the pursuit of happiness, and people's notions of happiness legitimately vary, as do the social, economic, and political barriers they face. To enable all to enjoy their basic rights securely, policies therefore must be not just resonant and respectful, but also reticulated. Governments cannot treat all persons in strictly uniform fashion. In deciding on public policies, American officials and citizens must engage in constantly changing contextual judgments about what accommodations for distinctive groups and identities will augment "the happiness and value of life" for all concerned—and what forms of differential treatment will instead foster divisions, inequalities, and injustices. Those judgments are difficult. They are also unavoidable if Americans are to respect legitimate differences in ways that further the best aspects of their common heritage and shared enterprise.

To make these policy judgments well, I have argued, Americans need to develop a new civic ethos, still built on the nation's Declaration of Independence project.[69] We must encourage all to pursue, among the diverse forms of happiness they may seek individually and as communities, those that are most valuable to others as well as to themselves—in part because those choices do most to permit and sometimes assist others in pursuing *their* distinctive forms of happiness. Many modern societies professing liberal democratic principles have defined justice in terms of John Stuart Mill's harm principle. It contended: "The only purpose for which power can be rightfully exercised over any member of a civilized community, against his will, is to prevent harm to others."[70] Modern Millians, wisely fearing that these harms will often be defined via the ethnocentric definitions of "civilized communities" that Mill himself often endorsed, adapt his harm principle along lines proposed by Ralph Waldo Emerson. Today, rather than speaking of the standards of "civilized communities," it is more customary to suggest that each person is entitled to the maximum amount of "self-defined" freedom and self-realization that is consistent with the self-defined freedom and self-realization of others.

This turn to protection of "self-defined" freedoms raises, however, a great danger. Persons pursuing diverse forms of self-realization may clash far more than they cooperate. To confront this danger constructively, we must first recall that today, even more than in the past, most people rightly recognize themselves as complex beings with many affiliations, interests, and aspirations, and thus many identities. They already are aware that they belong to many groups to which they feel some sense of allegiance, and that they might belong to still more. I have suggested that this awareness can make people feel they are being inundated by a cacophony of identity stories, increasing the attractiveness of simple, narrow, nationalist appeals—India First! America First! Yet that same awareness may inspire people to embrace more reticulated forms of public life, within their own societies and across societies.

It might enable many persons to see that they can seek self-realization in many different ways—ways that might be equally satisfactory to them, but have better or worse consequences for others. To show respect for those others, all of us should take such consequences seriously. I have therefore suggested that in pursuit of their Declaration of Independence project, Americans should adopt a modified Millian maxim as both a personal and a civic ethos. Members of other modern societies might do so as well, in ways that fit their distinctive histories and trajectories.

This modified maxim is: "The *best* uses of their powers by communities and individuals are those that aid others, without doing harm to themselves." Both to meet their own needs and goals and to do right by their fellow citizens in the twenty-first century, Americans need to go beyond simply trying to prevent harms. To be sure, efforts to combat harms, including disabling forms of discrimination, subordination, and material hardship, must remain central. Those efforts will continue to be hard, and they will continue to generate clashes over what constitutes "harm" and who is responsible for harms. Yet it still makes sense for citizens to strive more consciously to exercise their rights, individually and as a nation, in ways that benefit others, not just themselves. Doing so means that at times, local, state, and national governments should establish accommodations and exemptions in public policies for certain distinctive individuals and groups, because doing so will not harm more conventional citizens and communities, and it will enable these less conventional ones to pursue happiness, as they define it, more successfully, and in ways more practically equal to "mainstream" opportunities. Instead of "live and let live," America and other modern nations need a civic ethos of "live and help live."[71]

Aided by this ethos, the American Declaration of Independence project, in particular, can become not only resonant and respectful. It can provide better guidance for appropriately reticulated policies and practices than more traditional understandings of the nation's principles now provide. Legislators and executives devising public policies, and courts adjudicating them, should apply this modified Millian maxim in response to the claims of a wide range of advocates for special exemptions and accommodations—including religious groups, linguistic, cultural, ethnic, and racial minorities, the poor, the disabled, women, LGBTQ persons and groups, children, the elderly, and more. Rather than regarding all special treatment as suspect, as is now the norm, American lawmakers and courts should reverse the burden of proof. They should reject the claims of groups to affirmative accommodations only when those denials are needed to achieve some compelling governmental purposes—which must be more than simple hostility to the groups in question, or a demand that they give the nation "total allegiance."

Though this shift may at first blush appear too radical to be acceptable, the reality is that many reticulated policies have long been so common that they go almost unnoticed. Even as other forms of differential treatment have been decried, these similar measures have rarely been thought to require justification. Public institutions like museums, zoos, parks, and transportation systems, like many private businesses, have often provided discounts for the elderly and for children. Public and private organizations have also routinely accommodated—and reinforced—class inequalities, by offering different levels of service depending on ability to pay. With only a bit more controversy, persons with disabilities have in recent decades been allowed extra time to complete required state achievement exams. And though today many public and private buildings are gradually moving toward restrooms open to all, that departure from reticulated policies, in which two sexes were provided different facilities, is what is novel, not the long-standing tradition of differential treatment in this as in many other regards.

That venerable reticulated policy raises a vital point. It may now be time for this tradition of gender-specific restrooms to change. Yet in general, to be truly inclusive and respectful toward all, public efforts at accommodation must include conservative religious groups, as well as displaced workers, new immigrants, long-disadvantaged minorities, and more. For many, this is the implication of the Declaration of Independence project today that may be most difficult to accept. There are many good reasons to worry that extensive accommodations will only heighten fragmentation and inequality, not promote an egalitarian, inclusive sense of common endeavor. That worry is compounded if accommodations to some, especially traditionally privileged groups, appear to come at the expense of opportunities for others.

In assessing how much weight to give this very appropriate concern, we should bear one fundamental safeguard in mind. If we believe in equal rights—if we accept that each group and individual should have rights that have comparable value, but not greater value, than those granted to other groups and individuals—then we may often find that the state has a compelling interest in denying a request (or demand!) for special rights and accommodations. Once a government provides an accommodation to any one group, it must provide something comparable to all groups who similarly claim that those accommodations are vital to their members' pursuits of happiness. An ethos of seeking to accommodate all as far as possible is also an ethos that rejects just as firmly all claims of special privileges available only to a few fortunate groups.

This means that both legislators and courts must ask what the consequences will be of granting, for example, exemptions from Affordable Care Act requirements not only to conservative religious groups and to corporations owned by small groups of religious believers, but to all entities who make similar demands—a position the Trump administration has endorsed.[72] If there are many such bodies, then the sum of accommodations may be too costly, both in dollars and in terms of their impacts on other public goals, to be acceptable. Similarly, if we repeal the 1954 Johnson Amendment to the tax code and permit religious groups to endorse political candidates, as President Trump has moved to do, we must allow all tax-exempt advocacy groups to endorse candidates. We cannot grant religious traditionalists full political speech rights and tax exemptions while denying one or the other to environmental or animal rights groups. It is not clear the Trump administration would support granting full political speech rights uniformly to all tax-exempt organizations. It would therefore have to give up on promising preachers they could endorse candidates from their pulpits with no loss of tax exemption privileges. Finally, if the refusal of fundamentalist religious cake designers to serve same-sex couples means that those couples will have few opportunities to purchase desirable cakes, or that they will face related material burdens, then it would be illegitimate to exempt those cake designers from general policies of nondiscrimination.

But if requests for accommodations really are confined to a small number of groups, businesses, and individuals, while the interests of those adversely affected by those accommodations can be met through relatively inexpensive alternatives, then it is wise and just to support those accommodations. I include conservative cake bakers, so long as they publicly advertise their policies in order to prevent demeaning confrontations with gay customers. Those advertisements are likely to cost the bakers business, creating pressures for them to change their policies over time. It is true that until those changes come, some gay couples who know they will not receive service in a particular shop may well feel their dignity and identities have been disrespected, even though they have lots of other places to purchase well-designed cakes. Yet if religious shopkeepers are compelled to provide service for ceremonies that violate their moral beliefs, they will equally feel their dignity and identities have been disrespected. So long as same-sex couples can receive respectful service from most other providers, a civic ethos of accommodations wherever possible calls for permitting religious bakers an exemption.

In sum, we should take seriously the claims for accommodations advanced by long-discriminated-against or neglected communities, *and* those put forth by groups experiencing new economic anxieties due to economic globalization, environmental regulations, technological innovations, and unresponsive public policies, *and* the claims of traditional religious and cultural communities whose feelings of threatened status have led them to embrace Trump's vision. If accommodations and exemptions stop short of permitting some to burden what modern Americans define as basic civil rights, or obstructing other compelling public goals, these accommodations may contribute to civic peace and heighten civic engagement, improving the prospects for many to pursue happiness in fulfilling ways. Perhaps paradoxically but fortuitously, the incredibly rich diversity of modern America makes it likely that so few groups will advance requests for any particular distinctive privilege that many can be safely granted.

These policies would, moreover, promote the flourishing of the sorts of diverse civil associations that many regard as America's best schools for citizenship. Such associations can help foster the civic ethos that Americans need. They are often great venues for developing habits of working cooperatively with others to pursue not just individual self-interests but also common goods. Through those pursuits, a wide range of economic and cultural communities, including midwestern farmers, public sector labor organizers, immigrant advocacy groups, fundamentalist Christians, militantly proud deaf culture groups, persons of mixed-race descent, families with transgender members, and many more, may all come to feel that they are truly part of the American political project. They might then work together to realize a vision of America as a pluralist but united nation that strives seriously and persistently to make meaningful enjoyment of the basic Declaration of Independence rights possible for all.

These are the reasons why I find a civic narrative of America as a people dedicated to realizing the principles of the Declaration of Independence for all a far more compelling and promising vision than Trump's America First story, or even the democratic stories of figures like Dewey, or Barack Obama's e pluribus unum story. Nevertheless, as its invocation on behalf of many very different positions throughout U.S. history shows, the Declaration of Independence provides no certain guides for addressing all of modern America's problems. It is also limited in ways that may lead many Americans to prefer a different account of their identities and purposes.

As I stated at the outset, even though I favor this story, my goal is not to offer it as "the" single conception of American civic identity to which all should give allegiance, much less "total allegiance." As the writer Chimamanda Ngozi Adichie has said in a widely viewed TED talk, the "danger of a single story" is that it can rob "people of dignity" by standing in the way of "our recognition of our equal humanity," with full awareness of our differences.[73] Instead, I hope to encourage others to identify and advance the better stories of peoplehood that most appeal to them. Then we can look for areas of common ground for resistance to injustices, and common paths for progress. It is not by all adopting any one story of peoplehood, but rather through many people advancing different stories, all saying that xenophobia, racism, misogyny, and religious bigotry are NOT who we are now as Americans, that the United States can become, not only more united, but the best that we can hope to make it. We must look for many stories that resonate, that are respectful, and that are reticulated, stories that provide secure places for as many diverse groups as possible in the networks that comprise our society and in the regional and global networks to which we can productively belong. By doing so, we may find that our stories have many harmonies, and that we can build bridges across our divides. If we build well, they will be bridges on which we all can stand, and from which we can all look out with new hope toward the future whose story we will write. Perhaps we can write, and tell, and live better stories of peoplehood than all the stories that have gone before.

Afterword
On Doubts That May Remain

Many readers may at this point be convinced that all our political identities are in significant measure human creations that are often subject to intense contestation. Most will probably accept that this contestation is carried on in part by advancing rival accounts of imagined communities, clashing stories of peoplehood. They will agree that the kinds of nationalism I have termed "pathological populisms" gain appeal from narratives that lionize "the people" and demonize evil elites. Many will grant that every populist narrative is colored and embroidered with contents expressing the particular cultural traditions, the already-established myths, and the historic triumphs and suffering of the constituencies—"the people"—that would-be leaders aspire to lead. And some will believe that those populist narratives need to be countered by more egalitarian and inclusive ones that can still hope to resonate widely.

Other readers, however, may not be able to share this last hope, and so they may doubt the value of all I have proposed. Some will remain unconvinced that stories of peoplehood really matter much in politics. To them I ask, why then do we find political actors advancing them everywhere—especially highly successful ones? And, is it really conceivable that people could voluntarily cooperate in large-scale, enduring enterprises without the shared visions of their collective endeavors that stories provide them? It will not suffice to say that they will cooperate entirely out of individual calculations of rational self-interest: they still always need an account of just what collective endeavor their calculations are leading them to cooperate in. Finally, I repeat the related but still more fundamental reason for the importance of these political identity narratives. The fact is that we have virtually no interests or aspirations that are self-interpreting, especially in regard to the complex activities that political life involves. We feel we have wants and needs, but those feelings need specific content that can show how they can be fulfilled. This guidance comes from the stories of ourselves and our communities we adopt. It is a feature of human existence so basic that, like the air we breathe, we are often not conscious of it until it goes sour.

Others more sympathetic to the foregoing arguments may still worry that the stories nationalist populists tell are intrinsically far more able to respond to current anxieties and resentments than the kinds of "better" stories of peoplehood I have delineated here. In form and substance, the populist stories are structured to be both resoundingly affirming and conveniently undemanding. They imply that a mechanical law determines a political people's fate: when corrupt elites govern, the people suffer. When the people themselves rule—or actually, when their champions do—all is well. That is because the people are, like the children who watch television's Mr. Rogers, great "just the way they are." Populist narratives suggest that the people need not change or grow, they need not shed their old practices or beliefs, and they need not strive to do better. They simply need to put into power people who know how great they are and who will look out for them (probably more fiercely than Mr. Rogers tended to do).

In comparison, what I have called "better" stories may seem instead to be worse—far less appealing, in both form and substance. They are not nearly so reassuring, and they are not nearly so undemanding. They are usually structured as historical teleological narratives. They stress contextual solutions to immediate concerns, but they do so while defining "solutions" by commitments to challenging long-term goals: deepening democracy, achieving a more perfect union, extending meaningful enjoyment of basic rights to all. They promise the possibility of progress, but only through difficult efforts over many decades.

They are, to be sure, far from entirely off-putting. The first criterion for good stories calls for political narratives to begin with people as they are and to articulate a vision of community identity and common purpose that resonates with their currently felt needs, values, affiliations, and aspirations. Good stories must be stories in which people see themselves, and their individual stories. I have suggested that in the United States and in other lands, there are inclusive, egalitarian stories that can meet this criterion, that many in those nations can see as their own.

But the second criterion insists on narratives that urge people to show basic respect to all of humanity, no matter how disturbingly different, even dangerous, some groups and their ways of life may appear to be, or may actually be. Most demanding, the third criterion insists on narratives that summon people to accommodate those differences as far as possible, by accepting reticulated policies that treat people in varying ways, in accord with their distinctive needs and values. The criteria collectively reject the notion that political leaders should give priority to those who are now dominant in their community, even though those groups generally believe strongly that they should be put "First." Why should people follow those who call them to join in a difficult journey, rather than leaders who promise to restore to them a glorious past? Why should people accommodate those they despise, or those they see as threats to what they most value? Is it realistic to think that the sorts of stories I am urging can win popular support now—or ever?

Three reasons convince me that the answer is yes, though victories are never guaranteed. The first is a practical political one. In a perfect democratic utopia, discussions might continue until people reached universal agreement, but politics in the real world cannot work that way. Achieving political success involves building coalitions that have sufficient numbers and/or other resources to win out over opponents, through electoral processes or, at times, by other means. Though the tide has been running the other way, in the years ahead, the prospects should improve for building winning coalitions that embrace inclusive, egalitarian conceptions of political community. In many societies today, the numbers of people who believe they will benefit personally from these sorts of conceptions of peoplehood, or who find them more attractive for other reasons, are on the rise. In the United States, younger voters are both more liberal than older ones, especially on cultural diversity issues, and increasingly likely to be identified and to self-identify as nonwhite. They are not drawn to narrow visions of national identity, and certainly not to white Christian nationalism.[1]

In many other parts of the world, young people are unhappy with their leaders and disillusioned with politics. Even so, they are confident that their generation will do better in alleviating problems like poverty, and in providing education and employment for all, not just some.[2] Their visions of what they want their societies to be are far more broadly beneficial than what they think their current leaders, including populist leaders, are pursuing, much less achieving. Many countries are also experiencing both increased immigration and secularization, developments that often provoke culturally conservative populist mobilizations, but that also provide constituents for building countering coalitions, again especially among younger community members.[3] So in many countries, the losers now may be later to win—for the people themselves are changing.

In any case, leaders of conservative nationalist populist parties, like all other leaders, cannot hope to sustain support forever only by telling compelling stories. After a time, they must produce at least some confirming results. They must credibly deliver on most of their main economic promises—all the more so as they face mounting resentments from those who feel politically disempowered under their governance. As I've noted, the unexpected poor performances of the mayoral candidates of President Recep Tayyip Erdoğan's nationalist AKP in the spring 2018 elections in Ankara as well as Istanbul were due in large measure to the country's declining economy, along with intensifying anger over Erdoğan's increasingly authoritarian rule.[4] Since all countries experience economic downturns, sooner or later in many places material conditions will provide opportunities for proponents of different national narratives to gain followers, so long as their narratives include economic policies as well as other themes that address economic hardships credibly. And in many countries, it may become more and more possible to oppose authoritarians with coalitions of those who want to gain or regain their political freedom.

Some readers may respond, ah, yes, but at least for the foreseeable future, it is more likely that continuing economic distress, increasing cultural diversity, and deepening political divisions will only permit nationalist populists to stoke fear and anger still higher, building coalitions strong enough to crush the champions of greater inclusion. Perhaps; but for how long?

The second reason to think that less chauvinistic stories of peoplehood can succeed is that most people, most of the time, actually prefer civil peace to culture wars, much less wars of physical violence. As Machiavelli argued centuries ago, though in every society there are those who long for power and domination, most people "have only the wish not to be dominated," and to be able to live their lives free of oppression and turmoil.[5] When they are convinced that they are suffering under corrupt elites, they can certainly be roused to ferocious support for populist leaders. Yet this is a psychological and political mood that is hard to sustain. It is draining to be incessantly called to hate and to fight. Over time, willingness to do so is likely to fade, especially if opposition leaders offer constituents less turbulent, more tranquil political paths that include visible respect for their interests and values. Even if stories of political purpose calling on people to "live and help live" may be heard as too demanding by some, they may still be drawn to accommodating policies offering hope that they and their neighbors can "live and let live," reducing experiences of strife and conflict in their daily lives.

The third reason puts this point more positively. Though people may enjoy hearing they are great just as they are, especially if they feel they have long been disregarded and dismissed, it is likely that most people do not entirely believe it. They think they can be better; they think they should be better; and deep down, they want to be better. My late father, a deeply conservative businessman without any real theological convictions, attended church every Sunday—religiously, so to speak!—to listen to mostly liberal mainline Protestant preachers. He did so for many reasons, some of them economic: being a good churchgoer was good for business. Yet he also once explained to me that he liked to hear what other thoughtful, decent people believed about what it means to be a good person on this earth today. Though others at our church were surely there more for the solace of feeling that they were loved by God, or to experience membership in a warm and welcoming community, most seemed just as glad as my dad to be called to become, and to be helped to become, more closely attuned to what they felt to be the better angels of their nature.

As members of a predominantly white, middle-class, largely native-born midwestern congregation, those Presbyterian churchgoers, members of the same denomination in which Donald Trump was raised, certainly were capable of resenting immigrants, fearing people of color, and feeling threatened by calls for more redistributive and egalitarian economic and social policies. But most were also capable of feeling ashamed about putting their own narrow self-interest above all else. They were capable of being proud that they could feel such shame.[6] And they were capable of feeling excited about forming better relations with, and sharing in making progress with, others who were disadvantaged, or who came from different cultures, or who simply had fresh ideas on ways we all could have better lives together. These aspects of their beliefs and their identities made them capable of responding to darker appeals by deciding, in the end, "that is not who we are." I believe that many people who sometimes long for the restoration of an older, more traditional society, nonetheless are still open to hearing stories of how they might make themselves, their neighbors, their country, and the world better going forward. In parts of their hearts, they want to believe those stories. When they feel they can believe them, they want to live those stories.

Thus it does not seem quixotic or hopeless to seek to devise better stories of peoplehood for those to whom we feel most closely connected, in the hope that they will be inspired by the prospect of a future that will be in vital respects new, and greater than anything so far, instead of responding to calls for a return to a once-great past. Instead, it seems much more quixotic to believe that a better future can be reached without such stories. Reverential as many conservative Americans are for their nation's past, even they often strive to gain support by promising they will help people to realize the American Dream in the future, rather than saying they will bring back the land of American Memories.

And in the end, the importance of stories of peoplehood is that they are the stuff that dreams are made of. It is true that dreams differ, and ones that some find beautiful are nightmares for others. But at a time when Cold War nightmares haunted the world even as new hopes were on the rise, a small-town midwestern American poet offered the promise that members of all political communities would be wise to offer to one another today: "I'll let you be in my dream if I can be in yours."

Notes

Introduction

1. For elaboration of this argument in relationship to political science in particular, see Rogers M. Smith, "Identities, Interests, and the Future of Political Science," *Perspectives on Politics* 2 (2004): 301–312; and see also Rawi Abdelal, Yoshiko M. Herrera, Alastair Ian Johnston, and Rose McDermott, "Identity as a Variable," *Perspectives on Politics* 4 (2006): 695–711. For a seminal sociological analysis, see Rogers Brubaker, *Ethnicity without Groups* (Cambridge: Harvard University Press, 2004).

2. Oliver Wendell Holmes Jr., "The Path of the Law," *Harvard Law Review* 10 (1897): 505.

3. See, e.g., Jo Wuest, "The Scientific Gaze in American Transgender Politics: Contesting the Meanings of Sex, Gender, and Gender Identity in the Bathroom Rights Case," *Politics and Gender,* July 27, 2018, 1–25, DOI: 10.1017/S1743923X18000338.

4. See, e.g., Aimi Hamraie, "Universal Design and the Problem of 'Post-Disability' Ideology," *Design and Culture: The Journal of the Design Studies Forum,* August 19, 2016, 285–309, DOI: 10.1080/17547075.2016.1218714.

5. Aron Hirt-Manheimer, "What Does It Really Mean to Be 'The Chosen People'?" ReformJudaism.org, May 22, 2015, https://reformjudaism.org/blog/2015/05/22/what-does-it-really-mean-be-%E2%80%9C-chosen-people%E2%80%9D.

6. See generally Eva Marie Garoutte, *Real Indians: Identity and the Survival of Native America* (Berkeley: University of California Press, 2003). Cf. Annie Linsky and Amy Gardner, "Elizabeth Warren Apologizes for Calling Herself Native American," *Washington Post,* February 5, 2019, https://www.washingtonpost.com/politics/elizabeth-warren-apologizes-for-calling-herself-native-american/2019/02/05/1627df76-2962-11e9-984d-9b8fba003e81_story.html?utm_term=.90ebf797f975.

7. For a critical overview by a census veteran, see Kenneth Prewitt, *What Is Your Race? The Census and Our Flawed Efforts to Classify Americans* (Princeton: Princeton University Press, 2013).

8. A recent collection of twenty-seven of Obama's most prominent speeches on all topics includes six such quotations, a rate of just over 22 percent of his addresses. See E. J. Dionne Jr. and Jo-Ann Reid, eds., *We Are the Change We Seek: The Speeches of Barack Obama* (New York: Bloomsbury, 2018).

9. Richard N. Haass, "The Age of Nonpolarity: What Will Follow U.S. Dominance," *Foreign Affairs* 87, no. 3 (2008): 44–56, 48, https://www.foreignaffairs.com/articles/united-states/2008-05-03/age-nonpolarity.

10. See, e.g., Maurice Charland, "Constitutive Rhetoric: The Case of the People Québecois," *Quarterly Journal of Speech* 73, no. 2 (1987): 133–150; Stuart Hall, "Ethnicity: Identity and Difference," *Radical America* 23, no. 4 (1989): 9–20; Andrew D. Brown, "A Narrative Approach to Collective Identities," *Journal of Management Studies* 43 (2006): 731–753; Arjo Klamer, "Visualizing the Economy," *Social Research* 71, no. 2 (2004): 251–262; Jennifer L. Erkulwater, "Constructive Welfare: The Social Security Act, the Blind, and the Origins of Political Identity among People with Disabilities, 1935–1950," *Studies in American Political Development* 32, no. 3 (2019): 1–29. For my arguments, Rogers M. Smith, *Stories of Peoplehood: The Politics and Morals of Political Memberships* (New York: Cambridge University Press, 2003), and *Political Peoplehood: The Roles of Values, Interests, and Identities* (Chicago: University of Chicago Press, 2015).

11. Benedict Anderson, *Imagined Communities: Reflections on the Origins and Spread of Nationalism* (New York: Verso, 1983).

12. Yuval Noah Harari, *Sapiens: A Brief History of Humankind* (New York: Harper Perennial, 2015), 27, 105.

13. Jeanne Morefield, *Empires without Imperialism: Anglo-American Decline and the Politics of Deflection* (New York: Oxford University Press, 2014), 3.

1
A Cacophony of Stories

1. Jan-Werner Müller, *What Is Populism?* (Philadelphia: University of Pennsylvania Press, 2016), 3–4.

2. Ibid., 101.

3. Ibid., 19.

4. Lawrence Goodwyn, *The Democratic Promise: The Populist Moment in America* (New York: Oxford University Press, 1976); Charles Postel, *The Populist Vision* (New York: Oxford University Press, 2007).

5. Cas Mudde and Cristóbal Rovira Kaltwasser, "Exclusionary v. Inclusionary Populism: Comparing Contemporary Europe and Latin America,"

Government and Opposition 48, no. 2 (2013): 149–150; Cas Mudde and Cristóbal Rovira Kaltwasser, *Populism: A Very Short Introduction* (New York: Oxford University Press, 2017), 6.

6. Giorgos Katsambekis, "The Populist Surge in Post-Democratic Times: Theoretical and Political Challenges," *Political Quarterly* 88, no. 2 (2017): 204–205.

7. Kirk Hawkins, Madeleine Read, and Teun Pauwels, "Populism and Its Causes," *The Oxford Handbook of Populism*, ed. Cristóbal Rovira Kaltwasser, Paul Taggart, Paulina Ochoa Espejo, and Pierre Ostiguy, 267–286 (Oxford: Oxford University Press, 2017), http://www.oxfordhandbooks.com/view/10.1093/oxfordhb/9780198803560.001.0001/oxfordhb-9780198803560-e-13.

8. For both types of arguments see ibid. For the cultural case, see, e.g., Pippa Norris and Ronald F. Inglehart, *Cultural Backlash: Trump, Brexit, and Authoritarian Populism* (New York: Cambridge University Press, 2019). For the economic case, see, e.g., Yann Algan, Sergei Guriev, Elias Papaioannu, and Evgenia Passari, "The European Trust Crisis and the Rise of Populism," *Brookings Papers on Economic Activity*, September 7–8, 2017, https://www.brookings.edu/wp-content/uploads/2017/09/4_alganetal.pdf. For an account that stresses economic factors over cultural ones but also highlights the senses of political powerlessness many are experiencing due to globalization, see Michael Cox, "Understanding the Global Rise of Populism," *LSE Ideas*, 2019, http://www.lse.ac.uk/ideas/research/updates/populism.

9. Hawkins, Read, and Pauwels, "Populism and Its Causes."

10. Viktor Orbán, "Speech at the 28th Bálványos Summer Open University and Student Camp," July 22, 2017, http://abouthungary.hu/speeches-and-remarks/viktor-orbans-speech-at-the-28th-balvanyos-summer-open-university-and-student-camp/.

11. Jane Louise Kandour, "President Erdoğan—A Patriot or a Nationalist?" *Daily Sabah*, December 5, 2018, https://www.dailysabah.com/feature/2018/05/12/president-erdogan-a-patriot-or-a-nationalist; cf. Meral Ugur Cinar, *Collective Memory and National Membership: Identity and Citizenship Models in Turkey and Austria* (New York: Palgrave Macmillan, 2015), 23–31.

12. Boris Johnson, "The Rest of the World Believes in Britain. It's Time We Did Too," *The Telegraph*, July 15, 2018, https://www.telegraph.co.uk/politics/2018/07/15/rest-world-believes-britain-time-did/; Rob Price, "Here's Boris Johnson's Full Resignation Letter: 'We Are Truly Headed for the Status of Colony,' " *Business Insider*, July 9, 2018, https://www.businessinsider.com/boris-johnson-resignation-letter-brexit-2018-7.

13. See, e.g., Sarah Song, "The Boundary Problem in Democratic Theory: Why the Demos Should Be Bounded by the State," *International Theory* 4, no. 1 (2012): 39–68.

14. See, e.g., Paulina Ochoa Espejo, *The Time of Popular Sovereignty: Process and the Democratic State* (University Park: Pennsylvania State

University Press, 2011); Rogers M. Smith, *Political Peoplehood: The Roles of Values, Interests, and Identities* (Chicago: University of Chicago Press, 2015), 216.

15. For pertinent discussions see, e.g., Margaret Canovan, *The People* (London: Polity, 2005); Bernard Yack, *Nationalism and the Moral Psychology of Community* (Chicago: University of Chicago Press, 2012).

16. Yuval Noah Harari, *Sapiens: A Brief History of Humankind* (New York: Harper Perennial, 2015), 28–34.

17. Ibid., 24–25, 27, 34, 103, 110.

18. Ibid., 26.

19. Ibid., 111–112. Cf. John Hutchinson, *Nationalism and War* (Oxford: Oxford University Press, 2017), 22 ("War-making is dependent not just on organization but on normative consent and motivations"); Rogers M. Smith, *Stories of Peoplehood: The Politics and Morals of Political Memberships* (New York: Cambridge University Press, 2003), 44 ("Warlords . . . always need at least some members who are persuaded to fight for them by words, not by arms alone").

20. Smith, *Stories of Peoplehood,* 56–60.

21. Smith, *Political Peoplehood,* 2; cf. Smith, *Stories of Peoplehood,* 19–20.

22. Smith, *Political Peoplehood,* 50–53.

23. Meral Ugur Cinar and Rogers M. Smith, "National-Building Narratives: Implications for Immigrants and Minorities," in *The Nation State and Immigration: The Age of Population Movements,* vol. 3, ed. Anita Shapira, Yedidia Z. Stern, Alexander Yakobson, and Liav Orgad (Brighton, UK: Sussex Academic Press and the Israel Democracy Institute, 2015), 6–11.

24. See, e.g., Beth Simmons and Zachary Elkins, "The Globalization of Liberalization: Policy Diffusion in the International Political Economy," *American Political Science Review* 98, no. 1 (2004): 171–189.

25. Philip G. Cerny and Alex Prichard, "The New Anarchy: Globalization and Fragmentation in World Politics," *Journal of International Political Theory* 13, no. 3 (2017): 378–394, 383.

26. Ibid., 380–383.

27. Francis Fukuyama, *Political Order and Political Decay: From the Industrial Revolution to the Globalization of Democracy* (New York: Farrar, Straus and Giroux, 2014), 187.

28. The most comprehensive survey by a political scientist remains Samuel E. Finer's magnum opus, written in retirement, *The History of Government from the Earliest Times* (Oxford: Oxford University Press, 1997).

29. For an array of examples and analyses see, e.g., Mahmood Mamdani, *Citizen and Subject: Contemporary Africa and the Legacy of Late Colonialism* (Princeton: Princeton University Press, 1996); Fukuyama, *Political Order and Political Decay,* 299–312; Francisco Garrido and Diego Salazar, "Imperial

Expansion and Local Agency: A Case Study of Labor Organization under Inca Rule," *American Anthropologist* 119 (2017): 631–644; Josep M. Colomer, "Empires v. States," *Oxford Research Encyclopedia of Politics,* June 2017, 6, DOI: 10.1093/acrefore/9780190228637.013.608.

30. Finer, *History of Government,* 1066–1076, 1261–1306, 1473–1566.

31. "Decolonization," *United Nations,* http://www.un.org/en/sections/issues-depth/decolonization/index.html; "Decolonization," *New World Encyclopedia,* http://www.newworldencyclopedia.org/entry/Decolonization.

32. John F. Kennedy, "Inaugural Address," The American Presidency Project, January 20, 1961, http://www.presidency.ucsb.edu/ws/index.php?pid=8032.

33. Francis Fukuyama, "The End of History?" *National Interest* 16 (1989): 3–18.

34. Richard N. Haass, "The Age of Nonpolarity: What Will Follow U.S. Dominance," *Foreign Affairs* 87, no. 3 (2008): 44–56, 48, https://www.foreignaffairs.com/articles/united-states/2008-05-03/age-nonpolarity.

35. Ibid., 45. See also Shaun Breslin, "Leadership and Followership in Post-Unipolar World: Towards Selective Global Leadership and a New Functionalism?" *Chinese Political Science Review* 2 (2017): 494–522.

36. Haass, "The Age of Nonpolarity," 45–46.

37. Greenpeace, "About," https://www.greenpeace.org/usa/about/.

38. Cited in Nadya Nedelsky, *Defining the Sovereign Community: The Czech and Slovak Republics* (Philadelphia: University of Pennsylvania Press, 2009), 195–196, 234–235.

39. Ibid., 194–220, 235–243.

40. David Frum, "The Toxic Politics of Migration in the Czech Republic," *Atlantic,* October 23, 2017, https://www.theatlantic.com/international/archive/2017/10/czech-elections/543669/.

41. Davide Lerner, "Why Slovakia Won't Embrace Migration: 'If Multiculturalism Is Failing in Places Like Paris and Brussels, Why Should We Try It Here?' " *Politico,* August 7, 2016, https://www.politico.eu/article/why-slovakia-wont-embrace-migration-lubos-blaha-josef-rydlo/.

42. Ibid., and "Migration in Slovakia," International Organization for Migration, https://www.iom.sk/en/migration/migration-in-slovakia.html; "Slovakia Immigration Detention," Global Detention Project, https://www.globaldetentionproject.org/countries/europe/slovakia.

43. Calvert W. Jones, *Bedouins into Bourgeois* (New York: Cambridge University Press, 2017), 38–39.

44. Ibid., 42–43, 46–47.

45. Ibid., 129–130.

46. Ibid., 48–62.

47. Quoted ibid., 60.

48. Ibid., 195.

49. Jan M. Padios, *A Nation on the Line: Call Centers as Postcolonial Predicaments in the Philippines* (Durham, NC: Duke University Press, 2018).

50. Ibid., 2–3.

51. Ibid., 32–87.

52. Peter Robert Gardner, “Ethnicizing Ulster’s Protestants? Ulster-Scots Education in Northern Ireland,” *Identities: Global Studies in Culture and Power* 25, no. 4 (2016): 397–416. Cf. “What Is Ulster-Scots,” on the website of the movement, Ulster-Scots Agency, at https://www.ulsterscotsagency.com/what-is-ulster-scots/.

53. Peter Robert Gardner, “Diaspora, Defeatism, and Dignity: Ulster Protestant Reimaginations of the Self through Ulster-Scots Americanism,” *Ethnic and Racial Studies* 41 (2018): 2048–2066.

54. Ibid., 2058, 2063.

55. Ibid., 2063.

56. Katherine J. Cramer, *The Politics of Resentment: Rural Consciousness and the Rise of Scott Walker* (Chicago: University of Chicago Press, 2016). For Cramer’s analysis of the support of those she studied for Trump, see Katherine J. Cramer, “The Competence of Others: Understanding Perceptions of Others’ Civic Abilities,” *items: Insights from the Social Sciences,* Social Science Research Council, July 25, 2017, https://items.ssrc.org/the-competence-of-others-understanding-perceptions-of-others-civic-abilities/.

57. Cramer, *The Politics of Resentment,* 23–24.

58. Ibid., 66–72, 165.

59. Breslin, “Leadership and Followership.”

60. Google, https://www.google.com/about/.

2
What Makes a Good Story of Peoplehood?

1. Yascha Mounk, *The People vs. Democracy: Why Our Freedom Is in Danger and How to Save It* (Cambridge: Harvard University Press, 2018), 197, 207–210.

2. William A. Galston, *Anti-Pluralism: The Populist Threat to Liberal Democracy* (New Haven: Yale University Press, 2018), 4, 66–71, 96, 117–119.

3. Francis Fukuyama, *Identity: The Demand for Dignity and the Politics of Resentment* (New York: Farrar, Straus and Giroux, 2018), 7–11, 142, 162, 166, 170–174, 178.

4. See generally David Ricci, *Why Conservatives Tell Stories and Liberals Don’t: Rhetoric, Faith, and Vision on the American Right* (Boulder, CO: Paradigm, 2011); David Ricci, *Politics without Stories: The Liberal Predicament*

(New York: Cambridge University Press, 2016). For a related analysis, see Eldon J. Eisenach, "Can Liberalism Still Tell Powerful Stories?" *European Legacy* 11, no. 1 (2006): 47–71.

5. In *Why Nationalism* (Princeton: Princeton University Press, 2019), Yael Tamir makes a compelling argument for the importance of advancing desirable forms of nationalism. The analysis here explores how to do so, in ways that avoid chauvinistic excesses now and that open paths for possible revisions in the existing system of nation-states in the future.

6. See, e.g., Michael Walzer, *Interpretation and Social Criticism* (Cambridge: Harvard University Press, 1993).

7. See, e.g., United Nations Population Fund, "Core International Human Rights Instruments," 2004, https://www.unfpa.org/resources/core-international-human-rights-instruments; Switzerland Federal Department of Foreign Affairs, "International Human Rights Conventions," September 11, 2018, https://www.eda.admin.ch/eda/en/home/foreign-policy/international-law/un-human-rights-treaties.html.

8. Publius [James Madison], *The Federalist No. 10*, in Alexander Hamilton, James Madison, and John Jay, *The Federalist Papers,* ed. Ian Shapiro, 47–53 (New Haven: Yale University Press, 2009), 48–49.

9. Marie Helweg-Larsen, "Why Denmark Dominates the World Happiness Report Rankings Year after Year," *CNBC Life,* April 16, 2018, https://www.cnbc.com/2018/04/16/why-denmark-dominates-the-world-happiness-report-rankings-year-after-year.html.

10. Christian Joppke, *Citizenship and Immigration* (Cambridge: Polity, 2010), 53, 61, 134–135; Richard Jenkins, "Citizenship, Belonging, and Identification: The State of Denmark," in *Narrating Peoplehood amidst Diversity,* ed. Michael Böss, 41–60 (Aarhus: Aarhus University Press, 2011), 57–58.

11. Søren Krarup, cited in Claus Møller Jørgensen, "The Writing of History and National Identity: The Danish Case," in Böss, *Narrating Peoplehood amidst Diversity,* 231–259, 245.

12. Kristian Thulesen Dahl, "The Party Program of the Danish People's Party," as established October 2002, https://danskfolkeparti.dk/politik/in-another-languages-politics/1757-2/.

13. Ibid.

14. "Denmark Personal Income Tax Rate," *Trading Economics*, https://tradingeconomics.com/denmark/personal-income-tax-rate.

15. "Party Program."

16. Ibid.

17. Jørgensen, "The Writing of History and National Identity," 232–233.

18. Ibid., 253; Ove Korsgaard, "Grand Narratives in Danish History: From Functional Identity to Problematic Identity," in Böss, *Narrating Peoplehood amidst Diversity,* 261–272, 263–264.

19. Jørgensen, "The Writing of History and National Identity," 249; Korsgaard, "Grand Narratives in Danish History," 264–269.

20. "Foreign-born Population," *OECD Data,* https://data.oecd.org/migration/foreign-born-population.htm.

21. Jørgensen, "The Writing of History and National Identity," 253–254; Korsgaard, "Grand Narratives in Danish History," 271.

22. Jenkins, "Citizenship, Belonging, and Identification," 54.

23. Jørgensen, "The Writing of History and National Identity," 247.

24. See, e.g., Staff and Agencies, "Denmark Passes Law Banning Burqa and Niqab," *The Guardian,* May 31, 2018, https://www.theguardian.com/world/2018/may/31/denmark-passes-law-banning-burqa-and-niqab; Emma Graham-Harrison and Janus Engel Rasmussen, "Stigmatised, Marginalized: Life inside Denmark's Official Ghettos," *The Guardian,* August 12, 2018, https://www.theguardian.com/world/2018/aug/12/denmark-official-ghettos-cultural-assimilation-country-once-tolerant; Jon Henley, "Danish Mayors Vow to Ignore Citizenship Handshake Plan," *The Guardian,* September 20, 2018, https://www.theguardian.com/world/2018/sep/20/danish-mayors-vow-to-ignore-citizenship-handshake-rule. I am grateful to Anders Berg-Sørensen for these references.

25. For a recent effort (in Danish) along these lines by a leading Danish Social Liberal, see Ida Auken, *Dansk* (Copenhagen: People's Press, 2018).

26. Manoj Mate, "Constitutional Erosion and the Challenge to Secular Democracy in India," in *Constitutional Democracy in Crisis?* ed. Mark A. Graber, Sanford Levinson, and Mark Tushnet, 377–394 (New York: Oxford University Press, 2018), 378–379.

27. Bharatiya Janata Party, "Election Manifesto 2014: Ek Bharat Shreshtha Barat, Sabka Saath, Sabka Vikas," http://www.bjp.org/images/pdf_2014/full_manifesto_english_07.04.2014.pdf.

28. Ibid.

29. Ibid.

30. Ibid.

31. Mate, "Constitutional Erosion," 386.

32. Ibid., 390–392; Jeffrey Gettleman, Suhasini Raj, Kai Schultz, and Hari Kumar, "India Revokes Kashmir's Special Status, Raising Fears of Unrest," *New York Times,* August 6, 2019, https://www.nytimes.com/2019/08/05/world/asia/india-pakistan-kashmir-jammu.html; Christophe Jaffrelot, "Toward a Hindu State? India Democracy at 70," *Journal of Democracy* 28, no. 3 (2017): 52–63, 54–57, 59, 61.

33. Mate, "Constitutional Erosion," 394.

34. NDTV, "Election Results 2014: 5 Factors that Helped BJP and Narendra Modi Win the Election," May 16, 2014, https://www.ndtv.com/cheat-sheet/election-results-2014-5-factors-that-helped-bjp-and-narendra-modi-win-

the-election-562309; Sunil Khilnani, *The Idea of India* (New York: Farrar, Straus and Giroux, 1997), 183–184; C. A. Bayly, "The End of Liberalism and the Political Thought of Nehru's India," *Modern Intellectual History* 12 (2015): 605–626, 624–625.

35. See, e.g., Louise Tillin, "Indian Elections 2014: Explaining the Landslide," *Contemporary South Asia* 23, no. 2 (2015): 117–122, 118, 120–121, and the articles in that special symposium issue.

36. Office of the Registrar General and Census Commission of India, "Religion," http://censusindia.gov.in/Census_And_You/religion.aspx; Al Jazeera, "Hindus Drop Below 80% of India's Population," August 26, 2015, https://www.aljazeera.com/news/2015/08/hindus-drop-80-percent-india-population-muslims-census-150826052655585.html; Gyan Varma, "BJP Is No Longer Limited to Specific Social Base: PM Modi," *LiveMint,* April 23, 2018, https://www.livemint.com/Politics/hyeH2ZDnSCh7qlZmpbNlFM/BJP-is-no-longer-limited-to-specific-social-base-PM-Modi.html; D. L. Sheth, *At Home with Democracy: A Theory of Indian Politics,* ed. Peter Ronald deSouza (Singapore: Palgrave Macmillan, 2018), 18–19.

37. Khilnani, *The Idea of India,* 2.

38. Ibid., 154–155.

39. Ibid., 159; Sheth, *At Home with Democracy,* 27–29, 36–38.

40. Bayly, "The End of Liberalism," 622, 626; Khilnani, *The Idea of India,* 154, 164–166; Sheth, *At Home with Democracy,* 29, 38–39; Luis Cabrera, " 'Gandhiji, I Have No Homeland': Cosmopolitan Insights from BR Ambedkar, India's Anti-Caste Campaigner and Constitutional Architect," *Political Studies* 65 (2016): 576–593, 579.

41. Khilnani, *The Idea of India,* 17.

42. Ibid., 167–176, 192; Sheth, *At Home with Democracy,* 39–44.

43. Cabrera, " 'Gandhiji, I Have No Homeland,' " 585–589.

44. Khilnani, *The Idea of India,* 36–37, 49–50, 181–183; Sheth, *At Home with Democracy,* 45, 256–262.

45. BW Online Bureau, "The Great India Debate: The Idea of India Needs to be Recreated," *Business World,* April 6, 2018, http://www.businessworld.in/article/The-Great-India-Debate-The-Idea-Of-India-Needs-To-Be-Recreated/06-04-2018-145700/.

46. See, e.g., ibid.; Peter Ronald deSouza, "Introduction: A Political Theory of Indian Democracy," in Sheth, *At Home with Democracy,* 16–19.

47. The Editors, "Netanyahu's Embrace of Far-Right Populists Risks Betraying Israel's Values," *WPR: World Politics Review,* January 10, 2019, https://www.worldpoliticsreview.com/trend-lines/27160/netanyahu-s-embrace-of-far-right-populists-risks-betraying-israel-s-values.

48. Meral Ugur Cinar and Rogers M. Smith, "Nation-Building Narratives: Implications for Immigrants and Minorities," in *The Nation State and*

Immigration: The Age of Population Movements, vol. 3, ed. Anita Shapira, Yedidia Z. Stern, Alexander Yakobson, and Liav Orga (Brighton, UK: Sussex Academic Press and the Israel Democracy Institute, 2014), 20–21.

49. Ibid.

50. Raoul Wootliff, "Final Text of Jewish Nation-state Law, Approved by the Knesset Early on July 19," *The Times of Israel,* July 18, 2018, https://www.timesofisrael.com/final-text-of-jewish-nation-state-bill-set-to-become-law/.

51. Ronald S. Lauder, "Israel, This Is Not Who We Are," *New York Times,* August 14, 2018, https://www.nytimes.com/2018/08/13/opinion/israel-ronald-lauder-nation-state-law.html. I chose the title for this book before Lauder's op-ed appeared, though it reinforced the choice.

52. Naftali Bennett, "Israel Is Proud of Who We Are," *New York Times,* August 15, 2018, https://www.nytimes.com/2018/08/15/opinion/israel-nationality-law-naftali-bennett.html.

53. In a similar vein, see the defense of "egalitarian Zionism" in Chaim Gans, *A Political Theory for the Jewish People* (New York: Oxford University Press, 2016).

54. Michael Krumholz, "Jorge Muñoz Elected Mayor of Lima," *Peru Reports,* October 7, 2018, https://perureports.com/jorge-munoz-elected-mayor-of-lima/8561/; Alejandro Telleria Torres, "Peru Elections: Right-wing Populism Defeated at the Polls," *WikiTribune,* https://www.wikitribune.com/article/90862/.

55. Ibid., and "César Acuña," *Peru Reports,* https://perureports.com/cesar-acuna/.

56. "Jorge Muñoz Wells Elected Mayor of Lima," UCCI: Unión de Cuidades Capitales Iberoamericanas, October 15, 2018, https://ciudadesiberoamericanas.org/jorge-munoz-wells-alcalde-electo-de-lima-tomara-posesion-del-cargo-el-1-de-enero-de-2019/.

57. "Does Péter Márki-Zay's New Movement Pose a Threat to Fidesz?" *Hungarian Spectrum,* February 28, 2019, http://hungarianspectrum.org/2019/02/28/does-peter-marki-zays-new-movement-pose-a-threat-to-fidesz/.

58. Marc Santora, "Sweeping Election Victory Gives Hungary's Ruler Control over Constitution," *New York Times,* April 9, 2018, https://www.nytimes.com/2018/04/08/world/europe/hungary-election-viktor-orban.html. But in October 2019, Fidesz candidates lost in Budapest and ten other Hungarian cities.

59. "Does Péter Márki-Zay's New Movement Pose a Threat to Fidesz?"

60. "Péter Márki-Zay: My Hope Would Be for a Technocrat Government," *VPost: Visegradpost,* April 6, 2018, https://visegradpost.com/en/2018/04/06/peter-marki-zay-my-hope-would-be-for-a-technocrat-government/.

61. Carlotta Gall, "Turkey's President Suffers Stinging Defeat in Istanbul Election Redo," *New York Times,* June 24, 2019, https://www.nytimes.com/2019/06/23/world/europe/istanbul-mayor-election-erdogan.html.

3
Who Are We Americans Now?

1. Samuel P. Huntington, *Who Are We? The Challenges to America's National Identity* (New York: Simon and Schuster, 2004).

2. Carlos Lozada, "Samuel Huntington, a Prophet for the Trump Era," *Washington Post,* July 18, 2017, https://www.washingtonpost.com/news/book-party/wp/2017/07/18/samuel-huntington-a-prophet-for-the-trump-era/?utm_term=.d3e03f86dd24.

3. Huntington, *Who Are We?* 46, 371n15 (citing his own earlier claim that the "political ideas of the American Creed have been the basis of national identity" while indicating he now thought it misleading).

4. Ibid., 49.

5. Ibid., 221–256, 357–362.

6. In his oral presentation, Trump added, and emphasized, the "only" and the repetition of "America first" to his official written text. Compare Donald J. Trump, "The Inaugural Address," January 20, 2017, https://www.whitehouse.gov/briefings-statements/the-inaugural-address/, with "Donald Trump's Inauguration Speech—Full Speech," https://www.youtube.com/watch?v=FFH7QMZ5N1k. Previously in the United States the "America First" slogan was most identified with Charles Lindbergh's call in September 1941 for the United States not to oppose Nazi Germany, a lineage Trump may not have known at first and that he has since ignored, despite press coverage highlighting it. Louisa Thomas, "America First, for Charles Lindbergh and Donald Trump," *New Yorker,* July 24, 2016, https://www.newyorker.com/news/news-desk/america-first-for-charles-lindbergh-and-donald-trump.

7. Kirk Hawkins, Madeleine Read, and Teun Pauwels, "Populism and Its Causes," *The Oxford Handbook of Populism,* ed. Cristóbal Rovira Kaltwasser, Paul Taggart, Paulina Ochoa Espejo, and Pierre Ostiguy, 267–286 (Oxford: Oxford University Press, 2017), http://www.oxfordhandbooks.com/view/10.1093/oxfordhb/9780198803560.001.0001/oxfordhb-9780198803560-e-13.

8. Trump, "Inauguration Speech," www.whitehouse.gov.

9. Donald J. Trump, "Remarks at Youngstown State University in Youngstown, Ohio," August 15, 2016, The American Presidency Project, http://presidency.proxied.lsit.ucsb.edu/ws/index.php?pid=119503.

10. Ibid.

11. Michael C. Bender, "Trump Strikes Nationalistic Tone in Inaugural Address," *Wall Street Journal,* January 20, 2017, https://www.wsj.com/articles/donald-trump-strikes-nationalistic-tone-in-inaugural-speech-1484957527?tesla=y&mod=e2tw.

12. David Leonhardt and Ian Prasad Philbrick, "Donald Trump's Racism: The Definitive List," *New York Times,* January 15, 2018, https://www.nytimes.com/interactive/2018/01/15/opinion/leonhardt-trump-racist.html.

13. Quoted in Jan-Werner Müller, "Donald Trump's Use of the Term 'the People' Is a Warning Sign," *The Guardian,* January 24, 2017, https://www.theguardian.com/commentisfree/2017/jan/24/donald-trumps-warning-sign-populism-authoritarianism-inauguration.

14. John Sides, "Race, Religion, and Immigration in 2016," The Democracy Fund Voter Study Group, June 2017, https://www.voterstudygroup.org/publication/race-religion-immigration-2016, 17.

15. Lynn Vavreck, "The Great Political Divide over American Identity," *New York Times,* August 12, 2017, https://www.nytimes.com/2017/08/02/upshot/the-great-political-divide-over-american-identity.html.

16. Leonhardt and Philbrick, "Donald Trump's Racism," and see generally John Sides, Michael Tesler, and Lynn Vavreck, *Identity Crisis: The 2016 Presidential Campaign and the Battle for the Meaning of America* (Princeton: Princeton University Press, 2018), esp. 201–220.

17. Charlie Savage, "Justice Dept. to Take on Affirmative Action in College Admissions," *New York Times,* August 2, 2017, https://www.nytimes.com/2017/08/01/us/politics/trump-affirmative-action-universities.html.

18. Conor Arpey, "The Business Implications of Disparate Impact's Uncertain Future," BLR Buzz Blog, *American University Business Law Review,* April 17, 2017, http://www.aublr.org/2017/04/business-implications-disparate-impacts-uncertain-future/.

19. Laurel Raymond, "Trump Administration Eliminates Funding for Group Countering White Nationalism," *ThinkProgress,* June 23, 2017, https://thinkprogress.org/white-nationalism-group-funding-f1d35fb5604e/.

20. Christopher Ingraham, "Here Are the First 10 Members of Trump's Voting Commission," *Washington Post,* July 6, 2016, https://www.washingtonpost.com/news/wonk/wp/2017/07/06/here-are-the-first-10-members-of-trumps-voter-fraud-commission/?utm_term=.abadedb44f38.

21. Emily Bazelon, "Department of Justification," *New York Times,* February 8, 2017, https://www.nytimes.com/2017/02/28/magazine/jeff-sessions-stephen-bannon-justice-department.html?_r=0.

22. Peter Baker, "Trump Supports Plan That Would Cut Legal Immigration by Half," *New York Times,* August 3, 2017, https://www.nytimes.com/2017/08/02/us/politics/trump-immigration.html; Michael Wines and Adam Liptak, "Trump Considering an Executive Order to Allow Citizenship Question on Census," *New York Times,* July 6, 2019, https://www.nytimes.com/2019/07/05/us/census-question.html.

23. Michael D. Shear and Julie Hirschfeld Davis, "As Midterm Vote Nears, Trump Reprises a Favorite Message: Fear Immigrants," *New York Times,* November 1, 2018, https://www.nytimes.com/2018/11/01/us/politics/trump-immigration.html.

24. For discussion and citations, see Rogers M. Smith, *Political Peoplehood: The Roles of Values, Interest, and Identities* (Chicago: University of Chicago Press, 2015), 206–209.

25. Daniel T. Rodgers, *As a City on a Hill: The Story of America's Most Famous Lay Sermon* (Princeton: Princeton University Press, 2018).

26. John Winthrop, "A Defense of an Order of the Court," in *American Political Thought: Four Hundred Years of Ideas and Ideologies,* ed. Sue Davis, 34–35 (Englewood Cliffs, NJ: Prentice-Hall, 1996); Rodgers, *As a City on a Hill,* 78–79.

27. Rodgers, *As a City on a Hill,* 200–201.

28. Cited in Smith, *Political Peoplehood,* 207.

29. Rogers M. Smith, *Stories of Peoplehood: The Politics and Morals of Political Membership* (New York: Cambridge University Press, 2003), 197–212.

30. See, e.g., Publius [James Madison], *The Federalist No. 10*, in Alexander Hamilton, James Madison, and John Jay, *The Federalist Papers,* ed. Ian Shapiro, 47–53 (New Haven: Yale University Press, 2009), 50–52.

31. See, e.g., John Dewey, *Reconstruction in Philosophy,* enlarged ed. (1920; Boston: Beacon, 1948), 186, 200–209.

32. Chantal Mouffe, *For a Left Populism* (New York: Verso, 2018), 62.

33. Ibid., 76.

34. Ibid.

35. Ibid., 71.

36. Ibid., 6, 45.

37. Ruth Braunstein, *Prophets and Patriots: Faith in Democracy across the Political Divide* (Berkeley: University of California Press, 2017).

38. Ibid., 176–178.

39. Ibid., 188.

40. Ibid.

41. Frances McCall Rosenbluth and Ian Shapiro, *Responsible Parties: Saving Democracy from Itself* (New Haven: Yale University Press, 2018); Publius [Madison], *The Federalist No. 10*, 53.

42. Robert Foa and Yascha Mounk, "Are Americans Losing Faith in Democracy?" *Vox,* December 8, 2015, https://www.vox.com/polyarchy/2015/12/18/9360663/is-democracy-in-trouble; Larry Diamond, "Are People Losing Faith in Democracy?" *American Interest,* March 16, 2018, https://www.the-american-interest.com/2018/03/16/people-losing-faith-democracy/.

43. "Obama 2004 Democratic National Convention Keynote Address," American Rhetoric, http://www.americanrhetoric.com/speeches/convention2004/barackobama2004dnc.htm.

44. Ibid.

45. "Barack Obama's Campaign Speech," *The Guardian*, February 10, 2007, http://www.guardian.co.uk/world/2007/feb/10/barackobama.

46. "Transcript of Obama's Speech on Race," NBC News, http://www.msnbc.com/id/23690567/print/1/displaymode/1098/.

47. "Remarks by the President at Cairo University, 6-04-09," at https://obamawhitehouse.archives.gov/the-press-office/remarks-president-cairo-university-6-04-09.

48. "Obama's 2012 Nomination Acceptance Speech," The American Presidency Project, http://www.presidency.ucsb.edu/ws/index.php?pid=101968.

49. "Obama's Second Inaugural Address," The American Presidency Project, http://www.presidency.ucsb.edu/ws/index.php?pid=102827.

50. Rogers M. Smith, "The Constitutional Philosophy of Barack Obama: Democratic Pragmatism and Religious Commitment," *Social Science Quarterly* 93 (2012): 1251–1271.

51. Lindsay Boerma, "Obama Reflects on His Biggest Mistake as President," CBS News, July 12, 2012, http://www.cbsnews.com/news/obama-reflects-on-his-biggest-mistake-as-president/.

52. Ben Rhodes, *The World as It Is: A Memoir of the Obama White House* (New York: Random House, 2018), 372.

53. Barack Obama, "Address at the Hiroshima Peace Memorial," May 26, 2017, AmericanRhetoric.com, https://www.americanrhetoric.com/speeches/barackobama/barackobamahiroshimaspeech.htm.

54. Ibid.

55. See, e.g., Ronald Reagan, "The Shining City upon a Hill," January 25, 1974, http://www.originofnations.org/books,%20papers/quotes%20etc/Reagan_The%20Shining%20City%20Upon%20A%20Hill%20speech.htm; Rodgers, *As a City on a Hill*, 137, 146.

56. Ted Widmer, "Where Does American History Begin?" *American Scholar*, September 1, 2008, https://theamericanscholar.org/where-does-american-history-begin/#.W706E2hKjIU.

57. Charles H. Cosgrove, "The Declaration of Independence in Constitutional Interpretation: A Selective History and Analysis," *University of Richmond Law Review* 32, no. 4 (1998): 107–164, 112; Garry Wills, *Lincoln at Gettysburg: The Words That Remade America* (New York: Simon and Schuster, 1992), 261.

58. For a brief overview, see Smith, *Political Peoplehood*, 133–144.

59. See, e.g., William M. Wiecek, *The Sources of Antislavery Constitutionalism in America, 1769–1860* (Ithaca, NY: Cornell University Press, 1977); Mark Tushnet, *Taking the Constitution Away from the Courts* (Princeton: Princeton University Press, 1999), 182–193.

60. Lysander Spooner, *The Unconstitutionality of Slavery* (1845; Boston: Bela Marsh, 1860), 37–38, available at http://www.lysanderspooner.org/works/.

61. Frederick Douglass, "The Constitution of the United States: Is It Pro-Slavery or Anti-Slavery?" March 26, 1860, BlackPast.org, https://blackpast.org/1860-frederick-douglass-constitution-united-states-it-pro-slavery-or-anti-slavery.

62. Cosgrove, "The Declaration of Independence in Constitutional Interpretation," 107, 112–113, 117–126.

63. E.g., Robert W. Johannsen, ed., *The Lincoln-Douglas Debates* (New York: Oxford University Press, 1965), 304.

64. For discussion of Lincoln's thought in comparison with Obama's, see Rogers M. Smith, "Lincoln and Obama: Two Visions of American Civic Union," in *Representing Citizenship,* ed. Richard Marback, 17–51 (Detroit: Wayne State University Press, 2016).

65. Abraham Lincoln, "Letter to Joshua Speed," August 24, 1855, http://www.abrahamlincolnonline.org/lincoln/speeches/speed.htm.

66. See, e.g., David Armitage, *The Declaration of Independence: A Global History* (Cambridge: Harvard University Press, 2008).

67. Abraham Lincoln, "Fragment on Government," in *Abraham Lincoln: Selected Speeches, Messages, and Letters*, ed. Harry T. Williams, 38–39 (New York: Holt, Rinehart, and Winston, 1957).

68. For valuable analysis and recommendations, see Josh Chafetz, *Congress's Constitution: Legislative Authority and the Separation of Powers* (New Haven: Yale University Press, 2017); Frances Lee and Eric Schickler, eds., *Report of the APSA Task Force Project on Congressional Reform* (2019).

69. For elaboration, see Smith, *Political Peoplehood,* 197–199, 202–205.

70. John Stuart Mill, *On Liberty,* ed. David Spitz (1859; New York: Norton, 1975), 10–11.

71. I am grateful to William Barclay Allen for this formulation.

72. Internal Revenue Service, Department of Treasury, and Health and Human Services, "Moral Exemptions and Accommodations for Coverage of Certain Preventive Services under the Affordable Care Act," October 7, 2017, https://s3.amazonaws.com/public-inspection.federalregister.gov/2017-21852.pdf.

73. Chimamanda Ngozi Adichie, "The Danger of a Single Story," National Geographic Learning, https://ngl.cengage.com/21centuryreading/resources/sites/default/files/B3_TG_AT7_0.pdf.

Afterword

1. Emily Badger and Claire Cain Miller, "How the Trump Era Is Molding the Next Generation of Voters," *New York Times,* April 2, 2019, https://www.nytimes.com/2019/04/01/upshot/trump-era-molding-young-voters.html;

Kim Parker, Nikki Graf, and Ruth Igielnik, "Generation Z Looks a Lot Like Millennials on Key Social and Political Issues," Pew Research Center, January 17, 2019, https://www.pewsocialtrends.org/2019/01/17/generation-z-looks-a-lot-like-millennials-on-key-social-and-political-issues/.

2. IPSOS Game Changers, "Understanding the Perspectives of Young People around the World," September 24, 2018, https://www.ipsos.com/en-us/news-polls/Gates-goalkeepers-youth-optimism.

3. Eduardo Porter and Karl Russell, "Migrants Are on the Rise around the World, and Myths about Them Are Shaping Attitudes," *New York Times,* June 20, 2018, https://www.nytimes.com/interactive/2018/06/20/business/economy/immigration-economic-impact.html; Pew Research Center, "The Age Gap in Religion around the World," June 13, 2018.

4. Carlotta Gall, "Political Quake Via Ballot Box Stuns Erdogan," *New York Times,* April 2, 2019, https://www.nytimes.com/2019/04/01/world/europe/turkey-erdogan-election-loss.html.

5. Niccolò Machiavelli, *The Prince and the Discourses* (New York: Modern Library, 1950), 35–36, 119, 122.

6. This fact justifies attention to white shame, even if it can sometimes be counterproductive. See especially Christopher J. LeBron, *The Color of Shame: Race and Justice in Our Time* (2013; New York: Oxford University Press, 2015).

Acknowledgments

This book draws on the 2018 Castle Lectures sponsored by the Yale University Program on Ethics, Politics, and Economics. I am grateful to EPE Program Director Frances McCall Rosenbluth, to EPE Registrar Kelli Anne Farnham, and all at Yale who made returning to my former academic home so enjoyable. I got valuable feedback both from old friends there, including Seyla Benhabib, Ian Shapiro, Stephen Skowronek, and Steven B. Smith, and from many new ones. I greatly benefited from the reports of two Yale University Press reviewers and from the excellent suggestions of Yale editor William Frucht and copy editor Dan Heaton. Calvert Jones, Nadya Nedelsky, Jan Padios, and Kathy Cramer graciously advised on my analyses of their works. Anders Berg-Sørenson and Troels Skadhauge taught me about Denmark, as Peter Gardner did about Northern Ireland. Devesh Kapur's suggestions and seminars at Penn's Center for the Advanced Study of India shaped my view of India. Sigal Ben-Porath has long educated me about Israel through her words and about human goodness through her deeds. My account of Donald Trump draws on my continuing work with Desmond King. Anne Norton provided excellent readings of each of the original lectures. Zachary Koslowski and Jack O'Neil were superb research assistants, and Zachary aided greatly with the figures. I presented some arguments at meetings of the

American Political Science Association; the Northeastern Political Science Association; the Matthew J. Ryan Center; the SSRC Project on Popular Sovereignty; and at Albany, Berkeley, University of Maryland–Baltimore County, Columbia, Colorado, Georgetown, Hunter College, Notre Dame, Swarthmore, and Syracuse. I am grateful for helpful discussions at all these venues. Mary Summers has improved my thinking on these topics and all else for more than thirty years, while also enriching life beyond work and beyond words. Though thoughts of my offspring motivated every moment, this is the first book I have written without any children still living at home to distract me. Consequently, all its shortcomings are more than ever my own.

Index

Figures are indicated by **boldface** page numbers.